AUGSBURG COLLEGE
LIBRARY - MINN

Date Loaned		
Feb 26 '49		

THE MAKING OF MODERN
Holland
A Short History

THE MAKING OF MODERN
Holland

A Short History

BY

A. J. BARNOUW
Columbia University

W · W · NORTON & COMPANY · INC · *New York*

Copyright, 1944, by
W. W. NORTON & COMPANY, INC.
70 Fifth Avenue, New York 11, N. Y.

A WARTIME BOOK
THIS COMPLETE EDITION IS PRODUCED
IN FULL COMPLIANCE WITH THE GOVERN-
MENT'S REGULATIONS FOR CONSERVING
PAPER AND OTHER ESSENTIAL MATERIALS

PRINTED IN THE UNITED STATES OF AMERICA
FOR THE PUBLISHERS BY THE VAIL-BALLOU PRESS

TO

My Wife

Contents

I.	FROM BARBARIANS TO BURGHERS	11
II.	UNDER FOREIGN RULERS	29
III.	SOCIAL FERMENT	49
IV.	REVOLT	63
V.	THE DUTCH REPUBLIC	81
VI.	DUTCH-ENGLISH RIVALRY	103
VII.	THE FRENCH MENACE	124
VIII.	THE GOLDEN AGE	138
IX.	THE PERIWIG PERIOD	153
X.	THE MONARCHY	173
XI.	THE AGE OF WILHELMINA	198
	INDEX	217

Maps

THE NETHERLANDS ABOUT 1550   *Between pages* 64–5
CONTEMPORARY HOLLAND   201
THE NETHERLANDS EAST INDIES   *Between pages* 208–9

CHAPTER I

From Barbarians to Burghers

EARLY MAN, all over the world, has recorded the story of his life in symbols of his mortality. Only by studying how he was buried do we conceive a picture, however vague and superficial, of how he lived. Modern archaeology has opened a book of revelation which has for its main theme the resurrection of the dead.

There are no written records of early life in the Low Countries, but the soil has disclosed that this swampy, wind-swept, and sea-menaced region has never been uninhabited since the late diluvial period. Race after race swept over the land from its arctic past down to the present day. We do not know their names; we know only the shape of their skulls, the tools that they used, the manner of their burial. There were the cup people who built mass graves of wood in the shape of beehives. There were the builders of the *Hunebeds,* huge megalithic tombs that are still conspicuous features of the landscape of Drenthe. There were tribes who buried their dead in hollowed-out tree trunks, others who cremated them and interred the urns containing their ashes. Age after age sent waves of migration from east to west, as if the tide of humanity were as irresistibly drawn toward the sea as the sea toward the land. Hitler's invasion of Northwest Europe is the latest upsurge of that eternally undulating human ocean.

It is not true, then, that dead men tell no tales. These prehistoric dead are better witnesses than the living. It is less easy to prove from biological traits of the present-day Dutch that prehistoric life in the Low Countries was a melting pot of races. Still, it is evident that the Dutch nation is, racially, not a homogeneous whole. The large majority, no doubt, is of Germanic origin, but there is an amazing variety within that stock. The Hollander of the low polder region in the west is a different type from the peasant in the Achterhoek, which is that part of the province of Gelderland that is closest to the German border. The Brabanter and Limburger, in the south, show small resemblance to the people of Friesland, and the Zeelander, again, is a type apart.

These differences are not due to variety in environment. The ramification of the stock is not a recent process, but a tenacious survival of prehistoric diversity. The Dutch in the north are Frisians, those in the east Saxons, those in the west and south Franks, and the marked differences among them are inherited traits that divided them no less distinctly when they first appeared upon the scene of history. They all speak some variety of the Germanic language—to be more specific, of that branch of it which the linguists call West Germanic.

It is impossible, of course, to draw sharp demarcation lines between them. They have mingled along their common boundaries, creating transition groups that bear the marks of Frisian and Saxon, of Saxon and Frank, of Frank and Frisian origin.

Remnants of another race are living among these Dutchmen of Germanic background. They belong to the Alpine or Kelto-Slavic stock, which inhabited the Low Countries before they were invaded by the Germanic tribes. In the Zeeland isles, where they were safe from hostile raids behind ramparts of turbulent water, they escaped extinction or absorption, and it is there that one still finds a type of people strikingly different from their longheaded, blond, and blue-eyed fellow countrymen. They are dark-haired, dark-eyed, less tall than the Frisians and the Franks, and brachycephalic.

Among the Dutch it is the popular belief that rape and seduction of Zeeland girls by Spanish soldiers were of common occurrence during the Eighty Years' War, and that a Mediterranean strain was thus instilled into the stock. But modern science has measured the skulls and studied the pigments of thousands of blond and dark-haired Netherlanders, and these features have revealed to the biologists that in the dark-eyed people of Zeeland an ancient race survives that in other parts of the Low Countries lost its entity by absorption in the stock of the Germanic invaders. South of the Rhine and the Maas, in the provinces of Limburg and Brabant, the effects of this absorption are still noticeable in a shorter stature and darker pigments than are found farther north in the Netherlands. A similar modification of the characteristic Germanic traits can be observed when one travels cross country from the North Sea coast in an easterly direction, the Saxons along the German border combining the short skull of the Alpine race with the blond hair and the blue eyes of the Teutons.

The Frisians were the first to appear on the scene of history. Twelve years before the birth of Christ their country was invaded by the Romans under Drusus, stepson of Emperor Augustus. The Saxons and Franks were not known to the Romans. The regions these tribes later occupied were then inhabited by a great many tribes, partly Keltic perhaps, partly Germanic, whose names were recorded by Tacitus. But of only a few of these do we know more than the name.

Roman penetration in these parts was more of an economic than a military character. The conquerors, to be sure, built roads, dikes, and bridges, dug canals to link rivers, erected forts and blockhouses to protect their lines of communication. But there was little hostility between the native tribes and the Roman intruders. The latter exacted a tribute of cowhides, which was usually paid without demur. Once in a while there was an uprising when a Roman administrator was too rapacious and demanded more than the customary levy. But the natives had no sense of being enslaved. Many served in the Roman armies, not under compulsion but as free men who were out for adventure, combat, and loot.

Roman traders moved freely and unmolested through the land, selling wares from Italy and products of Roman workshops in Gaul and on the Rhine. The Frisians lived on manmade mounds on which they were safe from floods and inundation. These terps, as they are called, are still a characteristic feature of the Frisian landscape. They have nearly all been excavated and have yielded convincing proof of the Roman traders' ubiquity. Shards of Roman pottery have been found in such abundance that they must be the remains of the common utensils of everyday life.

Until about the middle of the third century peace and quiet seem to have prevailed in the valley of the lower Rhine. Roman culture affected every phase of native life in this region. From their rulers, the natives learned new techniques in architecture, stockbreeding, agriculture, gardening, art of writing, medicine, administration, commerce, household arts. The visible remains of that Roman past are but few. The castelli the Romans built have long since crumbled, the foundations of their roads and bridges have been obliterated, and if they erected any boastful monuments in the land of the vanquished, time has corroded the visible tokens of their pride. It is only the language that has preserved audible evidence of the power and the glory that were Rome's in the Low Countries. Its vocabulary contains a large number of words that the Germanic ancestors of the Dutch learned from their Roman masters. The man in the street will not suspect their Roman origin, they sound so thoroughly Dutch. But the linguist can trace in the Hollander's speech ineffaceable reminders of the cultural gifts that Rome brought to the Dutch eighteen centuries ago.

After A.D. 300 the power of Rome began to crumble along

the northern fringes of her empire. The pressure of migration from the east, which had been stemmed by the legions along the Rhine, grew in force as the military resistance weakened. The Frisians were the vanguard of this Germanic push toward the sea. They had reached the sea long before the arrival of the Romans. But now other hordes moved up out of the dark, mysterious forests of Germania. The diversity of tribes that Tacitus knew was obliterated in the welter that ensued. They became merged in larger tribal units. Only the Frisians showed their stamina by not letting the tide of migration sweep them off their feet. They stayed where they were and took neighboring tribes under their wings. Thus Frisian became the name of all who lived along the North Sea coast as far south as present-day Belgium. A vanguard of the Saxon nation settled on the sand and bog ground east of the IJsel River. The Franks were the master race among the invading hordes. They pushed on, across the Rhine and the Maas, where cultivated land and rich estates were for the taking, and turned this Gallo-Roman region into a Franconian state in which they were the ruling and landowning class.

In 496 King Chlodowech of the Franks was converted to Christianity. As a matter of course the king's example was law to his followers. Baptism was henceforth considered an act of common obedience, refusal to accept it an act of rebellion. The Frisians were still pagans two centuries later. Around the year 700 the gospel was brought to them by Willibrord, a native of Northumbria. He can hardly have felt a foreigner among them. His Anglian ancestors had come to Britain, in the fifth century, from homesteads in Northwest Germania that were near the Frisian borders. Angles and Frisians were closely related and spoke languages that came from a common stock. Willibrord understood their temper, for it resembled his own, and that, undoubtedly, was the secret of his success.

Part of that success, indeed, was due to the protection he received from Pepin, the ruler of the Franks. When the latter died in 714 King Radbod of the Frisians destroyed the churches that Willibrord had founded and restored the worship of his ancestors. But this was an act of revolt against Frankish supremacy rather than proof of his hostility to Willibrord's teaching. He identified Christianity with Frankish rule, and struck a blow at that rule by destroying churches. But he did not oppose Willibrord for what he taught. An early legend presents Radbod with one foot in the baptismal font. "Shall I meet my heathen ancestors in Christ's heaven?" he asked. The missionary shook his head: "They have gone to hell." "I'd rather go to hell and be with my ancestors than live in heaven among Christians," said Radbod and withdrew his foot. He did not hate Christianity, he was willing to embrace it, but not if baptism involved breach of faith to his forebears and submission to the ruler of the Franks.

After Radbod's death, Willibrord could resume his mission work under the powerful protection of Pepin's son Charles Martel, by whom the Frisian nation was incorporated with the realm of the Franks. The Saxons resisted the introduction of Frankish rule and Christianity more stubbornly. They had never been touched by Roman culture, and held to their pagan beliefs and their ancestral ways of life with greater tenacity. Charlemagne finally subdued them early in the ninth century, and Christianity was forced upon them with ruthless severity.

The mighty empire of Charlemagne fell apart after his death. The central power was lacking that could maintain its unity. In 843 his three grandsons divided their heritage by the Treaty of Verdun. Charles would rule in the west—that is, in the France that was to be—Louis in the Germanic east, and Lothair in Italy and the narrow buffer state between France and Germany. But this middle realm had no permanence. It was built out of disparate parts that stretched from the North Sea to the Mediterranean. Its northern half, including the Low Countries, fell to Lothair's second son and namesake, from whom it took its name Lotharingia. This was incorporated in 925 with the eastern realm, the German part of the old empire, and when Otto I of Germany conquered Italy, which gave him title to the imperial throne, the Low Countries became automatically a part of the Holy Roman Empire. Not all of them, though. In the southwest, the Dutch-speaking region between the Scheldt and the sea was added to the western realm. The political boundary between France and Germany tore the Low Countries apart.

It is highly doubtful whether the inhabitants minded this amputation. A Dutch nation did not yet exist. People's loyalties were given to local lords, to the soil they lived on, to the town of which they were burghers. The very name Dutch that binds them together was not yet in use.

Dutch is derived from an old Germanic word that meant people. The Anglo-Saxon missionaries were the first to refer to the language of the native tribes as the speech of the peoples, and by peoples they meant pagans, just as in Latin the plural *gentes* was used for the heathen. The new coinage passed from the reports of the missionaries into the chancelleries of the German Empire, and was finally adopted by the peoples themselves when their conversion to Christianity had emptied the word of its pagan implication. It proved a useful term, for it gathered the many tribal dialects under one head, and marked them the common speech of the people as distinct from Latin, the language of the church.

It mattered little to the common folk under what sovereignty they belonged. Life was wretched under any ruler. Western Europe under the later Carolingians was a scene of chaos. Pirates from Scandinavia terrorized the sea coasts of France and the Low Countries for nearly two centuries. All that the people could think of was how they could save their possessions and their lives. The marauders sailed up the rivers, laid inland towns in ashes, carried the inhabitants off into slavery, and left smoldering homes, famine, and death in their wake.

The chroniclers of that period paint a harrowing picture of the depth of demoralization to which the people of the Low Countries had sunk in their serfdom. "This region," says Thietmar von Merseburg, "is justly called the Low Countries, for justice, obedience, love for one's fellow-man sink low as the sun."

But like the sun they rose to a new dawn. Out of the welter a new order evolved after the fury of the Viking raids had abated. Great evils necessitate countermeasures that often turn out to be greater blessings. The *comites,* or counts, who were charged by the central government with the defense of the outlying provinces against the marauders, built strongholds along the coasts and at the mouths of rivers. A follower of the count was put in command of each castle. As the empire grew weaker, the counts grew more independent, the more so as they could rely on the loyalty of these military commanders whom they regarded as their vassals. With the help of the latter, the counts gradually restored order in the territories under their rule, and with the return of settled conditions, industry and commerce began to produce wealth. Traders and craftsmen sought security under the protection of these forts, which grew in course of time into ports and towns. The Dutch name for such a stronghold was *burgh,* that is, borough, and all those who were living under its protection were its *burghers.*

The merchants in these settlements formed, from the very beginning, a class apart. The towns were, in origin, of an agrarian character. The servants of the commander who made up the garrison and the workers who plied their several crafts were natives of the rural locality. The merchant class was recruited from various elements. They were often aliens whom the trade current had carried to the North Sea coast. They banded together, out of self-protection, into a guild or hansa, traveled in company to the annual fairs in other towns, looked as a group after their common interests, and by common action tried to gain a decisive voice in the administration of their towns. They were the most prosperous class: they imported from England the wool the weavers needed for their looms, they exported the cloth the weavers produced; they had charge of the flow of trade along the Rhine between upper Germany and Britain. They grew, at last, so powerful that their class interests became identified with those of the towns. What was best for the merchants was best for the entire community. Through their wealth they could impose their will upon their fellow burghers and challenge the authority of the feudal lords who used to be the military guardians of the boroughs.

Those feudal lords still acted as guardians, to be sure, but no longer against foreign raiders. Feuds among themselves often disturbed the peace the country had won from the Vikings. Commerce was injured by these outbreaks of civil war. Then the merchants would appeal to the count for help against his unruly vassals, and the count was more than willing to come to their aid. For it was to his interest to gain the wealthiest class of burghers as allies. He needed their money as much as they needed his protection. He would grant them privileges that freed their commerce from obnoxious restrictions imposed upon it by their feudal lords, or which had grown automatically from feudal conditions. In this way the merchant class, like a butterfly that sheds its cocoon, disengaged itself from the *burgh's* feudalism, whose protective shell it had needed in the initial stages of its growth. Since the borough's commerce was its very life blood, greater freedom for the merchants meant greater freedom for the town. Thus town and commerce together outgrew the bounds of feudal society. Though the lord of the borough still occupied the castle, he was no longer the sole arbiter of its destinies. Its military function had become subordinate to its commercial importance. As a member of the warrior class, that is, as a nobleman by birth, he was the sole aristocrat in a community of burghers; and in time of war that status gave him power and prestige. But when there was peace in the land the rich merchants were the real rulers of the borough, and the privileges granted to the borough by the count were calculated, as a rule, to protect and promote commerce and strengthen the power of the merchant class. Peace, therefore, was a social condition for which the lords of the boroughs, the barons one might call them, prayed with less fervor and sincerity than did the merchants. But the count, who proclaimed his peace throughout the land, as the church, around the year one thousand, had proclaimed the *Pax Dei*, the peace of God, would punish severely the vassal who dared to break it.

This was the course of development first in Flanders, subsequently in Holland, Brabant, and Gelderland, and in the diocese of the Bishop of Utrecht. For the latter was a secular lord in the province surrounding his seat and in a large tract of land east and north of the IJsel River. The ruler of Brabant was heir to the title of Duke of Lower Lotharingia, but as he never succeeded in enforcing his authority on the full extent of that territory, he was content to restrict his political ambitions within the boundaries of Brabant, without renouncing, however, his claim to the ducal title. The Count of Gelderland, thinking himself not inferior in power to his Brabant neighbor, obtained in 1339 from his liege lord, the German emperor, the elevation of his county to a duchy.

In Friesland there was no hereditary ruler. The Frisians never submitted to one central authority. They rather obeyed the local headman, to whom they gave allegiance with the same stubborn tenacity with which their heathen ancestors had given it to their tribal chieftains. The Count of Holland and the Bishop of Utrecht both tried to bring them under their authority, and this rivalry aided the cause of Frisian independence. When the Frisians were attacked by the count, they could always count on the bishop's aid, and vice versa. Expeditions against the unyielding Frisians became a chivalrous sport in which young squires could prove their mettle and gain the accolade of knighthood. These raids often ended in disaster. Count William II of Holland was badly defeated by the Frisians in 1256 and lost his own life into the bargain. Adventurous Englishmen who took part in another raid, in 1396, brought back atrocity stories of Frisian cruelty to their prisoners of war. There is an echo of these in a late ballade by Chaucer. Said the poet to his friend Bukton, when he wanted to dissuade him from marrying:

> And yf that hooly writ may nat suffyse,
> Experience shal thee teche, so may happe,
> That thee were lever to be take in Frise
> Then eft to falle of weddyng in the trappe.

Since Lower Lotharingia had been incorporated with the German Empire, its various counts and dukes were vassals of the emperor, except the Count of Flanders, who owed allegiance to the King of France. This was a misfortune for Flanders. For the emperors, always hard pressed to maintain their prestige in Italy, had no time or interest to spare for the enforcement of their authority in the Low Countries. They could not even maintain it effectively in the center of the realm; how then could they enforce it along its fringes? But the kings of France were jealous overlords. They insisted on more than lip-served allegiance, they wanted to rule Flanders in effect, and would allow the count no greater prestige than was due him as the king's governor in his Flemish fief.

The counts did not always resist these encroachments. Their speech and manners were French, and among the Flemish nobles and the ruling burgher families were many who spoke French and aped French fashions. These were willing to condone, even to support, a spineless subservience to the king's interference in the affairs of Flanders. But it was bitterly resented by the common people, especially by the large laboring class of the boroughs, the cities of Ghent, Bruges, and Ypres. The most numerous among these malcontents were the weavers of cloth, an ancient industry that already in Carolingian days had been selling its frieze, as the cloth was called, all over western Europe. The industry was dependent for its wool on the imports from England. Good relations with England were a requisite for the prosperity of Flanders and her laboring class. Hence the weavers saw in the King of England their natural ally against the King of France, and in the wars between the two monarchs the Flemish burghers were apt to side with the enemy of their count's liege lord. The count's authority was bound to suffer whichever cause he espoused. If he supported the popular one, he incurred the wrath, and often the revenge, of the King of France; if he played the part of loyal vassal, he incurred the hatred of his own people.

The counts of Holland could not escape becoming involved in these international conflicts. Every upheaval in the one county had its repercussions in the other. When Guy of Dampierre, Count of Flanders, conspired with King Edward I against France, the French king, Philip the Fair, found in Count Floris V of Holland a willing ally. But the English king too had his partisans in the county of Holland. Floris had wisely followed the policy of curbing the power of his unruly barons by increasing, through the bestowal of privileges, the freedom and the strength of the boroughs and their burghers. The opposition of the resentful nobles was easily turned into a pro-English faction. Floris was murdered in 1296. But the respite that Flanders obtained through his death was only temporary. The military aid she received from King Edward did not amount to much. Highborn and patrician partisans of France impaired the strength of Flemish resistance. By the end of the thirteenth century the county had been reduced to a mere province of the kingdom, and the count was a prisoner in France.

But the king did not long enjoy the fruits of his triumph. In 1302 the Flemish people rose up in revolt against the Francophile traitors in their midst, whom the king had put into power. A French army descended upon Flanders to restore order. But the Flemings, this time, were a match for the French. In the neighborhood of Kortrijk (Courtray) they defeated the enemy. The flower of French chivalry perished ignominiously on Flanders fields.

That victory of Dutch burghers over the king's army was a turning point in the history of the Low Countries. It gave the urban democracy a sense of its own strength and awakened in the people not only of Flanders but also of Holland and the rest of the Low Countries an awareness of their Dutchness which made them a community that was different from the French. Political frontiers did not mean much in those days. People were not taught geography in school and never looked at a map. They knew that the Count of Holland owed allegiance to the emperor, and the Count of Flanders to the King of France. But they saw in these feudal ties a purely personal relationship that meant little to them and concerned them less. If the Flemings, a century earlier, had been told that as inhabitants of a royal fief they were subjects of the King of France, they would have shrugged their shoulders and said, "What of it?" They were burghers of Ghent, of Bruges, of Ypres, and that was all that mattered. But after the battle of Kortrijk such unconcern was no longer possible. The fourteenth-century Fleming would hotly deny French citizenship and proudly proclaim himself a Fleming, and the growth in the other counties and duchies of a similar pride in independence from king or emperor heralded the awakening of Dutch nationalism.

On the surface little seemed to have changed as a result

of the Flemish victory. The count retained his power but swore anew allegiance to the king, made the cities do likewise, and bound his subjects to pay a heavy tribute by way of penalty for their disloyalty to the sovereign, as though the latter and not they had been the victor. The old relationships were automatically resumed, as if the burghers were politically not yet ready to dispense with the feudal ties which on the battlefield they had torn to pieces. But Flemish democracy was soon to come of age, and raise from its midst a mighty leader who would carry himself as an equal of kings, conclude treaties for his people with foreign powers, and challenge the might of France in defiance of the count, who remained faithful to his royal master.

Jacob van Artevelde was a wealthy cloth merchant of Ghent. He belonged to the urban patriciate of Flanders, but he came to power as the spokesman not only of his own privileged class but of the rank and file of the burghers. The Flemish nation stood behind him as a man, and the count, Louis of Nevers, fled like an outcast to Paris. It was Artevelde who persuaded King Edward III to press his claim to the French crown; it was at Ghent that Edward assumed the title of King of France; as the leader of the Flemish democracy Artevelde made Flanders Edward's ally. Off the port of Sluis the French fleet was annihilated by the allies in 1340. France was humbled a second time. The people's self-rule in Flanders seemed secure, in the future, from French interference. And Artevelde was worshiped throughout the county like a god.

But the worship was of brief duration. For the unity among his Flemish followers did not outlast the victory for long, and that unity was the foundation of his power. When the foundation cracked and fell apart his power tottered. Bruges and Ypres were jealous of Ghent, the rural population protested against the prohibition of weavers' looms outside the city walls, the weavers' and fullers' guilds waged war upon each other in Artevelde's own city. As soon as his foreign policy began to suffer reverses, the spell of his greatness was broken. When Edward withdrew from the continent without refunding the loan he had borrowed in Flanders, the embittered people of Ghent were as intemperate in cursing as they had been in blessing their leader. A mob of weavers invaded Artevelde's home, and the deacon of their guild slew him with the stroke of an ax.

But Artevelde had not lived in vain. The story of his life became a legend that was to inspire later generations of burghers and give them self-confidence in the maintenance of their freedoms. Civic liberty, indeed, was born and fostered in the towns and cities of the late Middle Ages. Urban life was the climate that was most favorable for its growth. The medieval peasant was hardly a free man. He was the dependent of some lord of the manor and exposed to his arbitrary commands. The townsman, on the other hand, was free, for he was subject only to the municipal government, which was composed of fellow burghers. The laws that governed the life within the walls of the borough made no distinction among burghers. They all enjoyed its protection in equal measure. Each town in a county, to be sure, had to recognize the count as master, the towns of Gelderland had to obey the duke, those of the diocese of Utrecht the bishop; and the towns could not with impunity disregard the laws of county, duchy, and bishopric. But their obedience was granted conditionally. For the counts and dukes, and the bishops as well, needed the financial support of the towns, and the burghers were willing to be taxed only in return for privileges in the grant of their overlords. Thus an even balance was struck between civil freedom and dynastic authority.

The Dutchman is by nature a rugged individualist. But rugged individualism does not make for civil liberty. On the contrary, it has a dissolving effect upon communal life and leads to anarchy. And outbreaks of anarchy were all too frequent in the medieval towns of the Netherlands. But the Dutch, who for various reasons, physical, economic, or political, joined their individual lives into communal units, learned by bitter experience that their strength lay in co-operation, and that co-operation was feasible only if all agreed to limit their personal liberties by common obedience to self-made laws.

The inhabitants of Holland and Zeeland had been induced by their age-long struggle against floods and inundations to organize for self-defense into small local units. That was the part nature played in training them for citizenship. Economic inducement to leave the land for the town was offered by the facilities for buying and selling that they now found in the town market. For an essential characteristic of an urban center, whether walled in or not, was its right to hold market. And finally, there was political advantage in being a townsman: one escaped from the arbitrary rule of a lord of the manor, who was often a petty tyrant, into the security of a local government, in which one had an interest and a voice.

The industrial and economic life of the town needed security for its undisturbed growth. Hence wall and moat became almost indispensable features of townships. Permission to wall in a community had to be obtained from the overlord, in Holland, Zeeland, and Flanders from the count, in Gelderland and Brabant from the duke, in Utrecht from the bishop. The charter under which the sovereign recognized a community's urban status defined the limits of the town's jurisdiction. These limits were not always identical with the walls. The town might have jurisdiction outside the walls, and where this was the case the extramural territory was called the town's Freedom.

The name testifies to the privileged position of the burgher in comparison with the peasant's status. The peasant who was so fortunate as to live in a town's Freedom was free from the arbitrary jurisdiction of the lord of the manor. The burgher and the husbandman within the Freedom were subject only to the town's jurisdiction. The *Jus de non evocando,* that is, the burgher's right to be tried in no other court than that of his own town, was an inviolable right which the city rulers were as anxious to maintain as were the burghers to invoke it.

By the end of the Middle Ages the majority of the Dutch people were living in urban centers. In 1500 the Low Countries, that is, the territory now embracing both Holland and Belgium, numbered no fewer than 208 fortified towns and 150 large villages which, but for the lack of walls, might pass for towns.

This preponderantly urban population was the bearer of Dutch culture. It is through international commerce that people grow intellectually and spiritually. The traders and merchants rubbed elbows with foreigners and learned from them better manners and new ideas. The towns attracted foreign craftsmen who often introduced new skills and techniques. There was a continuous ferment in city life that made for change and development. Rural life was conservative to the point of stagnation.

Dutch literature of the Middle Ages reflects the urban character of social life in the Low Countries. It is the expression of the burgher point of view, of realistic common sense and practical wisdom. Didactic and satirical verse was the burgher's favorite reading. The beginnings of Dutch poetry were, indeed, aristocratic. The French romances of chivalry were translated into Dutch and eagerly read not only among the nobility but also, doubtless, by the well-to-do burghers. But as burgher pride mounted and the political expansion of France became a menace, these stories of knightly adventure became unpopular. The poet Jacob van Maerlant started out as a narrator of romances of chivalry, but as he grew older he turned away from fiction and French falsehood, as he called it, and taught his countrymen in rhyming verse the scientific knowledge then available to man. Willem, the Flemish poet of the beast epic of Reynard the Fox, was also doubtless a member of the burgher class and shared its hatred of feudal arrogance and prerogatives. He took his plot from one of the many branches of the French Reynard cycle, but handled the borrowed material so deftly and with so much freedom and originality that the adaptation is universally conceded to be the best specimen of the genre in any language. It was a genre that suited the Dutch temper. It gave ample scope to a burlesque portrayal of human life and parodied with subtle humor the aristocratic romance of chivalry. The Dutch burghers enjoyed a story in which King Noble the lion and other beasts endowed with physical strength were duped by the cunning of little, defenseless Reynard. The poet had a sneaking love for his foxy hero, and felt no qualms of conscience in recounting his escapes from the punishment which from an ethical point of view he fully deserved. For he saw in his Reynard an emblem of burgher intellect triumphing over the arms of feudalism.

CHAPTER II

Under Foreign Rulers

THE HEREDITARY rulers did not look with disfavor upon the growing power of their burgher subjects. For their own power grew with it. Louis of Nevers had, as a faithful vassal, sided with the King of France against the Flemish cities, and that unwise policy, based on an outworn concept of feudal loyalty, had proved his undoing. Where the count and the burgher communes were allies, each party fared the better for the other's support.

Petty rulers they were, indeed, in respect to the size of their fiefs; but thanks to the geographical position of their lands at the mouths of the Rhine, Maas, and Scheldt, they were desirable allies to the most powerful monarchs of the age. Such alliances, however, though gratifying to their pride and ambition, were often expensive luxuries. They could not keep up with kings and emperors without the financial backing supplied by the cities. For it was from these that the bulk of their revenue came.

The matrimonial ties that bound these petty dynasties to the reigning houses of England, France, and the Empire prove that their political prestige was out of all proportion to the limited extent of their territories. Such marriages were moves on the political chessboard of the continent. The royal houses of England and France were constantly maneuvering for position, and royal brides supplied the bribes with which political advantage was secured. In the Hundred Years' War between France and England the hereditary rulers of the Low Countries were political profiteers. Marriage negotiations with one court promptly elicited a matrimonial offer from the other. In that way Louis the Bavarian's son, Duke Albert, who governed Holland, Zeeland and Hainaut (1358–1404) for his insane brother William V, induced Philip the Bold, Duke of Burgundy, to marry his son John to Albert's daughter, and John's sister to Albert's son and heir, Count William of Ostrevant.

The latter marriage was to prove the entering wedge for the House of Burgundy's intrusion into the northern Netherlands. It was already firmly entrenched in the south. Duke Philip himself had married the daughter of Louis of Male, Count of Flanders, and succeeded his father-in-law at his death in 1384. He had also won a foothold in the duchy of Brabant. For his wife was a niece of the Duchess Joanna, whose marriage with Wenceslaus of Luxemburg, brother of the Emperor Sigismund, remained childless, and she had her aunt's promise of the succession to the duchy.

William of Ostrevant, who succeeded his father as Count of Holland, Zeeland, and Hainaut in 1404, died thirteen years later, leaving as sole heir a daughter, the Countess Jacoba (1417–1433). His brother-in-law, Duke John, nicknamed the Fearless, of Burgundy, was murdered in 1419, and was succeeded by his son Philip, who was to win for himself the name of the Good. Philip's cousin Jacoba never saw much goodness in him. For eight years he schemed, intrigued and waged war against her until he finally succeeded in supplanting her.

He found good fishing in troubled waters. Holland was torn apart by civil war. The two warring factions were called the Codfish and the Hooks. The Codfish recruited their main forces from the towns of Holland, the Hooks, who were out to catch the cod, were the party of the nobility. But the motives for alignment with one faction or the other were often confused. There were noble houses that sided with the Cods and towns that supported the Hooks for some obscure reason. Jacoba's father had sided with the Hooks and banished the leaders of the Cods. He felt more at home in his native county of Hainaut, where French culture and the traditions of French chivalry gave glamor to his court, than in his two northern counties of Holland and Zeeland. The aristocrat in him made him espouse the cause of the nobles. But it was a political mistake on his part to antagonize the towns, and his daughter had to suffer for it. He made yet another by marrying Jacoba to Duke John IV of Brabant, as this match strengthened the Burgundian dynasty's hold on her inheritance. For John was the son of a younger brother of Jacoba's Burgundian mother.

The Emperor Sigismund watched the steady northward expansion of Burgundian power with growing concern. For the Low Countries, except for Flanders, were fiefs of the empire, and the emperor's authority was bound to suffer if a powerful French dynasty were to entrench itself on the lower Rhine. The Duke of Burgundy was sure to prove a defiant vassal and an additional element of corrosion in the already badly disintegrated realm. In order to thwart the Burgundian policy he promised his fiefs of Holland and Zeeland to Jacoba's uncle, John of Bavaria, a younger brother of her father. He hurried to Holland as soon as the news reached him that Count William VI had died in Hainaut, and headed a revolt of the Codfish against Countess Jacoba.

She tried in vain, with the help of her young husband, John of Brabant, to stem the tide. She was forced to sign an agreement under which her uncle John, together with her husband, would govern her three counties on her behalf. But the Duke of Brabant's partnership was no safeguard for Jacoba's interests. He did not attempt to protect them but let her uncle do as he pleased. John of Bavaria was the actual ruler.

It seemed as if Emperor Sigismund's anti-Burgundian policy had triumphed. But the instrument he had employed so successfully slipped from his grasp and became a tool in the hands of the enemy. John of Bavaria held sway at The Hague, far from the imperial court but close to Flanders, where Philip the Good of Burgundy had succeeded John the Fearless. Duke John saw greater safety in having the mighty neighbor for a friend than in having the distant emperor for a sponsor.

While the man who was to rescue the emperor's Dutch fiefs from Burgundian control was running over into the opponent's camp, Jacoba, intrepid and resourceful beyond her years, succeeded in disentangling herself from the Burgundian net. The church did not sanction a marriage between first cousins. The pope had granted dispensation from that ban in her case, but had revoked it at the emperor's insistence. Jacoba, on the strength of this cancellation, proclaimed herself illegally married and, consequently, free from the matrimonial tie with John of Brabant. She fled to England, hoping to counterbalance the power of her Burgundian cousin by marrying into the royal house of Lancaster. She had fixed her choice on Humphrey of Gloucester, brother of King Henry V. He married her in 1422, and John of Bavaria, seeing his position as her regent endangered, drew ever closer to Philip the Good, whose interests he believed to be identical with his own.

Jacoba's English husband did not prove the chivalrous champion of her rights she had hoped he would be. He invaded Hainaut, but soon returned to England and let Jacoba conduct her campaign alone. She was forced to surrender in 1425 and was imprisoned in Philip's castle at Ghent.

Her uncle John did not pluck the fruits of her defeat. He was poisoned that same year and left the county of Holland in a state of turmoil. Duke John of Brabant, who refused to admit the illegality of his marriage, tried to assume control as the husband of the captive countess, but, being a weakling, he failed to make his authority felt. He found it easier to call in his cousin, Duke Philip of Burgundy, and hand to him the reins of government. Philip had at last forced entrance into the coveted castle of Holland.

Jacoba made one last and desperate comeback. She escaped with her lady in waiting, both in page boys' disguise, from the prison at Ghent and made her way into Holland. The Hooks welcomed her with great rejoicings. Discontent among the suppressed elements of Holland's population and Dutch aversion to foreign rulers brought her additional allies. English forces also came to her assistance, but were utterly routed by the Burgundian troops. She still kept up courage and hope, appealing to her husband for fresh aid. But in 1428 the pope declared their marriage illegal, and Duke Humphrey, to the indignation of public opinion in England, turned its dissolution into a welcome pretext for leaving Jacoba in the lurch. That same year she was forced to recognize Duke Philip as her lieutenant governor and heir. Five years later he demanded and obtained her abdication. She died in 1436, in her thirty-fifth year.

Thus the Duke of Burgundy, in defiance of the emperor, and in spite of English opposition, had embattled himself in the Rhine delta, a position that gave him great strategic and economic advantages. He now controlled the entire coast line from the Frisian islands in the north down to Boulogne on the English Channel. The county of Hainaut had shared, for more than a century, the destinies of Holland and Zeeland and fell to him along with these. Brabant also belonged to him, since the younger brother and successor of Jacoba's husband John IV had died without heir in 1430. In 1456 he got his bastard son David appointed bishop of Utrecht. Luxemburg was added to his realm when Duchess Elisabeth, the widow of Jacoba's uncle John of Bavaria, died without issue. Philip's son Charles, who succeeded him in 1466, seized control of the duchy of Gelderland. By inheritance, marriage, intrigue, and force the dukes of Burgundy gathered in their grasp a large part of Lower Lotharingia, that fragment of the Carolingian Empire which, in the late ninth century, had been incorporated with Germany. It was their ambition to recover the full extent of that ancient realm.

The dukes of Burgundy were scions of the royal house of France. But the king's power had declined during the disastrous wars with England, and the Burgundian dukes, indifferent to their ties with the dynasty, were gradually building up a large and powerful state that would become a rival and a threat to the kingdom. Duke Philip had been an ally of the King of England against France, and that partly explains the halfhearted support Jacoba received from her English husband. The court in London could not reject an offer of marriage that gave it a foothold on the opposite coast, but as long as England was at war with France, there was wisdom in not thwarting his Burgundian ally's ambitions in the Low Countries.

In the conflict between Philip and Jacoba one's sympathies are naturally with her. One cannot help admiring the indomitable courage of the young countess who, true to the spirit of her chivalrous father, defended her rights against mighty odds. But she stood up for a lost cause. Our reason recognizes in the shrewd and calculating Philip the representative of a new age. Jacoba was a feudalist, and the days of feudalism were numbered. She did not realize the potential power that was inherent in the urban democracies, and put her trust in the support of the nobility and the lower classes, two very unruly elements that were incapable of organized and concerted action. For family feuds divided and weakened the one, lack of cohesion the other. The cities always favored the ruler who was able to enforce his authority and keep both the quarreling nobles and the rural proletariat in check. Philip, therefore, was their man, and the good that they saw in him was not goodness of heart but his fitness for maintaining order.

It does not follow, however, that the towns, for all their love of ordered conditions, did their best to maintain these themselves. Each town was still an isolated little world within its walls, just as each county and duchy was a self-assertive little island jealously guarding its insularity from the encircling sea of different life, laws, and manners. There were hatred, suspicion, envy, and strife within the national compass, just as there were in medieval Italy. National unity was still far to seek, and the willingness to find it was not apparent. It was only the Burgundian duke, as sole ruler over this political diversity, who was eager to weld those many interests into one nation.

Man's destinies are guided along mysterious ways that are seldom of his own choosing. Here were people of one common speech who seemed predetermined for nationhood. But they could not create it of their own free will. An outsider, a foreign ruler who could not speak their language, set himself to the task of forging them into a nation. He was not prompted by any love for the Low Countries. He loved them only for the strategic and economic advantages he could derive from them. His own country was Burgundy, and to make Burgundy the equal in power of France and the Empire was the ambition of his life. He cared for the Netherlands only in so far as they could serve him in the realization of his ambitious dream. Hence the unity he desired for them and did his best to bring about was merely a means to his own ends. Yet the people who resisted the unification that was forced upon them from the outside were, in the end, to be the only gainers. But that end was still far off and would not be reached until the Dutch had learned through suffering and tragedy the desirability of the goal.

In 1465 Philip the Good summoned a meeting of delegates from all the Low Countries and presented to them his son

Charles as his appointed regent. Such a convocation of the States-General was nothing new. In the preceding century these assemblies, made up of representatives of the nobility, the clergy, and the towns, had sometimes met for the discussion of common interests. But Philip introduced an innovation when he addressed to the meeting a so-called *bede,* that is, a request for a levy. Taxation until then had been the concern of each separate county, and the States of the several territories looked on the granting of such requests as their special prerogative. To have the matter submitted to them not as delegates from one province but as representatives of the realm that encompassed them all was an earnest of further encroachments by the composite state on the independence of its component parts. The delegates were accustomed to deal with their count or duke or whatever title the provincial ruler bore; they were now asked to deal with him as their collective sovereign.

Under the rule of Duke Charles (1465–77) the signs of a centralizing tendency multiplied. The States-General were asked for levies that were needed for the upkeep of bands of mercenaries which, in time of war, would serve as the nucleus of the duke's armed forces. Until then each separate state had raised, from among its populace, a contingent of armed citizens for the maintenance of peace within its borders and for the support of its ruler on his military expeditions. A standing army not raised from among the ruler's subjects but maintained at their cost for the safety of the whole was not a popular institution. Twice, in 1471 and 1473, they granted the request reluctantly, but in 1476 they turned it down.

The treasured *Jus de non evocando,* palladium of local independence, was imperiled by the establishment, in 1473, of a central Court of Last Resort, which soon evinced an alarming tendency to adjudicate cases in first instance; and the offices of the provincial comptrollers were subordinated to a central Chamber of Accounts, which, together with the Supreme Court, was established in the city of Mechelen.

In the separate provinces the duke, who was absent most of the time, had himself represented by stadtholders, each assisted by a council which in Holland bore the name of Court of Holland. These councils were copies on a smaller scale of the Privy Council that assisted the duke himself in the administration of his far-flung dominions. The personnel was recruited from among the nobility and the burgher jurisprudents trained in the universities of France, or in that of Louvain, the only institute of higher learning in the Netherlands. Knowledge of the law was a greater asset in these councils than noble birth and aristocratic manners, and the burgher members, consequently, became, in course of time, the backbone of the ducal administration. They formed a new aristocracy, the *noblesse de robe,* whose arms were intellect and expert knowledge.

The last vestiges of the feudal state had vanished from a regime whose administration largely depended on the loyalty of learned commoners. The ruler whom they served, though in name a vassal of the Emperor and the King of France, rejected all royal and imperial claims to his allegiance, and carried himself as an absolute monarch. The outward forms of feudalism were still preserved, and became more and more showy and pretentious as the system they symbolized came nearer and nearer to the stage of dissolution. At the institution of the Order of the Golden Fleece in 1430 Philip staged a magnificent pageant that made participants and onlookers think that the days of chivalry had come back in full glory. The occasion was his marriage with Isabella of Portugal, and the scene was the Flemish city of Bruges. Extravagance was the keynote at the wedding feast. Extravagant also was the concept of the Order. It bound the highest nobility of his lands together into a mystic brotherhood. The golden fleece worn on a chain around the neck was the badge of membership. To be included was to be the highest honor any nobleman of his realm could attain, and the knights of the fleece, like modern Argonauts, were to follow their Jason of Burgundy on a new crusade to the Holy Land which would test to the utmost their virtue, courage, and loyalty.

The political intrigues and military exploits of Charles the Bold that led to his downfall centered round his Burgundian homelands. They seldom affected, except indirectly, the course of events in the northern Netherlands. Still it is clear from what happened there after his death that the rule of the foreign duke was bitterly hated. When the news traveled north that Charles had fallen in a disastrous encounter with the Swiss at Nancy, the States-General intimidated Duchess Mary, his daughter and heir, into signing a document, known by the name of Great Privilege, under which she promised to respect the existing rights, privileges, customs, and usages, and concede the illegality of all government ordinances that ran counter to these; to dissolve the Supreme Court at Mechelen, and revise the constitution of the Privy Council in accordance with their wishes; and to be satisfied with military aid from the various states for such wars only as they themselves approved and were willing to help her wage.

The individual States also urged their private demands. Holland and Zeeland obtained from Duchess Mary a separate Great Privilege, by which she guaranteed, among a long list of promises, that in the future all ducal officials employed in the two provinces would be natives of these, and that in all documents addressed by the duchess to her subjects she would make use of the Dutch language.

These privileges, extorted from Mary in her helplessness, embodied pious wishes of the Dutch people that neither she nor her successors took seriously. Their value to the Dutch was not in any gain of greater freedom. But it gave them satisfaction to have formulated clearly the points at issue between themselves and the foreign dynasty. Mary's son and successor, Philip the Fair, treated his mother's promises as so many scraps of paper, but he could not tear the will to freedom which had dictated those points from the people's hearts. Again and again they would press their demands, until in the sixties of the next century, the pressure broke all restraints and the exasperated nation rose in revolt.

Philip the Fair (1478-1506) was Mary's son by Maximilian of Hapsburg, who in 1493, eleven years after his wife's death, was elected emperor. In 1496 Philip married Joanna, daughter of Ferdinand of Aragon and Isabella of Castile. Four years later a son was born to them at Ghent who was destined to become the ruler of the larger part of Europe. For Charles succeeded his maternal grandfather as King of Spain in 1516, and was elected emperor when the imperial throne fell vacant through the death of his father's father Maximilian. The succession in the Burgundian lands, including the Low Countries, fell to him in 1506 by the early death of Philip the Fair. He subsequently added to these the land of the unruly Frisians, the secular territory of the Bishop of Utrecht, and last, but not least, the extensive duchy of Gelderland, which he reconquered in 1543.

These later acquisitions remained under Charles V distinct from those that Philip the Good had acquired, a century previously, in that they did not send delegates to the States-General. The earlier gains formed a nuclear group. They were looked upon, in the sixteenth century, as the patrimonial provinces. The new additions did not take rank with these, nor were they particularly anxious to be included. They had submitted to the conqueror, but did not care to join the federation of his territories.

Nor did Holland, though one of the patrimonial provinces, feel herself very closely attached to the others. When Charles V, in 1534, proposed that the provinces should combine into a close-knit union which, like a hedgehog, would oppose its quills to the hostile world around, Holland refused to join on the ground that "in case of a war with France, all the taxes levied in Holland would go to the other provinces." The states of Holland would rather "make an alliance," they said, "with Brabant, Friesland, Overijsel, and Utrecht," of which Brabant alone was a patrimonial dominion. Here was the first suggestion of a federation of the northern provinces, such as actually came into being with the Dutch Republic of the Seven United Netherlands.

This cleavage between north and south was accentuated by the obvious preference that the Burgundians showed for the southern provinces. They held court at Ghent, at Brussels, at Mechelen, but never at The Hague or any other northern town. Charles V, like his predecessors, had himself represented in the northern provinces by stadtholders, one for Holland, Zeeland, and Utrecht, one for Gelderland, one for Friesland, Groningen, Drenthe, and Overijsel. They were always chosen from among the highest nobility of the southern Netherlands, whose speech and manners and general culture were French. They were as a rule out of sympathy with the less refined burghers they had to govern and could not make themselves popular with their master's subjects.

Still, the master did his best, in spite of native opposition, to fuse north and south into a centralized state. The policy initiated by the Burgundian dukes was continued with admirable consistency and perseverance. The central government was reinforced with a Council of State, and the Privy Council, now made up exclusively of jurisprudents and in session every day of the week, became the principal organ of the administration. The members of the Council of State were all noblemen of the highest rank, who were consulted by the monarch or, in his absence, by his regent, on matters of general policy.

Flanders, as we saw, and also the county of Artois, were fiefs of the King of France. Charles V had as little intention as his Burgundian forebears had shown to live up to the obligations that his vassalage involved. But disregarding them did not satisfy his pride; he wanted to see them abolished. Elimination of all French claims to part of his Burgundian patrimony would knit the Low Countries more closely together into an integral whole. His successful campaigns against King Francis I provided him with the opportunity that he had been looking for. Among the trophies he brought home from these was the release of both fiefs from their allegiance to the French monarch.

Although he happened to be emperor himself, Charles was no less anxious, as heir of the Burgundian dukes, to assert for the Low Countries a virtual independence from imperial obligations. As emperor he invited the Netherlands to send deputies to the imperial diets, and his sister, who ruled there in his absence, refused, not without his approval, to comply with the request. At the Diet of Augsburg, in the year 1548, he persuaded that assembly to recognize the unity of his Dutch possessions and to declare them free from imperial jurisdiction. They were at the same time, it is true, officially incorporated with the empire, of which they were to form the tenth, or Burgundian, *kreis,* or circle. This arrangement guaranteed them the protection of the Reich against foreign attacks, in return for a certain tribute that the kreis was to pay to the imperial treasury.

The incorporation was little more than a farce, as Charles V intended it to be. A nose of wax was the Dutch phrase: you could twist it and turn it into whatever shape you liked. The Netherlands treated it as a mere scrap of paper. They never sent delegates to the Diet, they never paid their share of the imperial taxation, they never asked to be protected by the Reich. As far as they were concerned the bond with the empire did not exist.

Consolidation and release from outside control were again the guiding motives that prompted the monarch to introduce a thoroughgoing reform of the ecclesiastical system in the Netherlands. All the provinces were subject to foreign archbishops: those of Cologne, Treves, and Rheims. The reform that was to emancipate them and unite them all under native supervision was the result of long-drawn-out negotiations with the pope. It was not introduced until 1559, in the fourth year of the reign of King Philip II (1555–98). Henceforth there were to be eighteen dioceses in the Netherlands, three of which, those of Utrecht, Mechelen and Cambray, were archbishoprics. All the bishops, except the Archbishop of Cambray, would be nominated by the monarch, who was determined to make his choice from among ecclesiastics with university training. The salaries of these prelates would be paid out of the income of a number of monasteries that were to be dissolved.

This was a very rational reorganization which made the Netherlands an ecclesiastical unit distinct and independent from any outside authority except that of the pope. Yet of all the reforms introduced with an eye to centralization this one aroused the greatest opposition from various elements of the populace. The monastic orders protested against the dissolution of convents, the high nobility against the appointment of scholars to episcopal sees; for ancient malpractice had taught them to look upon the emoluments from these as the lawful prey of members of their caste. And the burghers, no matter of what persuasion, suspecting that the new bishops were destined to be provincial inquisitors, foresaw the beginning of a general hunt for heretics with all the cruelties and horrors that went with it.

The Low Countries were a fertile soil for the seeds of heretical beliefs. The Dutch, as we said, are rugged individualists. They like to form their own opinions and reason things out for themselves. That tendency makes the average Dutchman a critical animal. The Dutch in the fifteenth century found much to criticize in their small world, and if there were abuses that escaped their observation, itinerant preachers would take good care to enlighten them by publicly castigating the morals of the age and denouncing the immorality then prevalent in high places, both secular and clerical. One of these preachers was Johannes Brugman, a Minorite friar who took the rule of St. Francis seriously. He adhered to the Observance, a reform movement within the order which sought to enforce the rule and make the members live up to the high standards of its noble founder. For immorality among the friars was open and unashamed. The repulsive picture that Chaucer painted of a mendicant was typical not only of conditions in England. All too many friars of that sort infested the Continent as well. In the fifties and sixties of the fifteenth century Brugman traveled widely through the northern Netherlands to spread the Observance and preach to the masses. His oratory must have made a deep impression on his hearers. Five centuries have not been able to efface the memory of it from the language. "To talk like Brugman" is still, in modern Dutch idiom, a familiar phrase expressive of persuasive eloquence.

He preached not only the tenets of the Observance but the blessings of a Christian life in general. He lived in a period of social upheaval, of strife between the classes, of stark contrasts between appalling poverty and vulgar display of wealth, of unbridled passions and shameless immorality in high places. But he had confidence in the stamina of the plain people. If these lived badly, their betters were to blame who did not give them a better example. By his preaching he tried to lead them back to decency and sober living.

Being a Franciscan, Brugman was imbued, at the start of his preaching career, with his order's prejudice against the Brethren of the Common Life, those simple friars who, unconnected with any monastic order and not adhering to any monastic rule, put the orders to shame by a pious life of obedience to God and service to their fellow men. But when he came to know them he admitted his error and conceived a deep and abiding admiration for them.

The founder of the brotherhood was Geert Groote of Deventer, where he was born in 1340. He studied in Paris, paying the cost of his studies with the income from a prebend in the diocese of Aix-la-Chapelle. He relinquished that benefice at his conversion, about the year 1375, to a life of the strictest self-discipline and mystical speculation. He often visited Jacob van Ruusbroec, the great Brabant mystic, for he admired the spirit of humility that prevailed in Ruusbroec's monastery in the country outside Brussels.

Groote practiced that Christian virtue in the conduct of his own life. He never deemed himself worthy to receive the consecration to the priesthood. But under license of the Bishop of Utrecht he preached before large multitudes throughout the northern Netherlands, exhorting them to follow in the footsteps of Christ. In his native town of Deventer he gathered around him a group of like-minded disciples, who formed a free community of brethren not bound by any monastic rules. They began to live together under one roof and called themselves the Brethren of the Common Life. Their House became the model of many similar fraternities, not only in the diocese of Utrecht, but in many others in the Netherlands and Germany.

By example and teaching Groote's brotherhood exerted a deep and lasting influence upon Dutch society in all its layers. The brethren and sisters—for there were also sororities —made piety and sober living popular. Parents were anxious to entrust their children's education to these devout men and women who sought union with God and salvation for their fellow men.

Mystics these brethren were, but in their devout search for God they never forgot their neighbors. The religious revival they brought to the Netherlands is known by the name of Modern Devotion. Their modernism lay in this combination of practical religion with the self-centered care for their own souls. The brotherhood was like a modern Mary who had chosen the good part which should not be taken away from her but who, at the same time, was willing to serve like Martha. And by that willingness to serve, the brethren gave meaning and beauty to the lives of thousands of their fellow men, both in the Netherlands and far and wide beyond its borders. For the brotherhood was not a learned caste. It entered the homes, the workshops, and the schools, and brought an element of devotion into the humdrum existence of the masses.

It also affected the tenor of monastic life. Though the brethren themselves did not constitute an order, they became instrumental in bringing about a monastic revival. For some followers of Geert Groote, preferring the discipline of the cloister to the greater freedom of the fraternities, withdrew to a monastery at Windesheim, south of Zwolle, and submitted themselves to the rule of the regular canons of St. Augustine, and a similar convent for women arose at Diepenveen near Deventer. In the course of the fifteenth century Windesheim became the model for many monasteries in various parts of the Netherlands and along the Rhine, which together formed a congregation that recognized Windesheim as its head. Nicholas Cusa, who visited the Low Countries in 1450 as papal legate, was so much impressed by the discipline and piety that prevailed in these Windesheim houses that he put them in charge of a monastic reform in a number of German bishoprics.

There is an intimate relationship between the writings that emanated from the Brethren of the Common Life and the *Imitatio Christi* of Thomas à Kempis. Thomas was a monk in a monastery not far from Zwolle, where he spent a long life in prayer, meditation, and the copying of manuscripts. He had his models, to be sure, in composing the *Imitatio* and used them with a freedom that, in our day, would not escape the charge of plagiarism. A German scholar, Dr. Paul Hagen, has brought to light an older version of the second and third books, which Thomas remodeled to suit his purpose, and Dr. J. van Ginneken has argued quite plausibly that this older version was from the hand of Geert Groote. The *Imitatio* is a composite work less expressive of an individual than a communal devotion, the purest and noblest record of that inner experience which the mystics of the IJsel Valley regarded as the real life.

The spirit of Geert Groote and his brotherhood pervaded Dutch life all through the fifteenth century, and bred in the Dutch that tolerance and true Christian charity which were to make the Dutch Republic a haven of refuge for the persecuted from other lands. Erasmus was never deeply attached to his native soil, and seldom had a word of praise for his compatriots. But in one of his Colloquies someone who has escaped from a shipwreck praises "the incredible humanity of the people, who with great alacrity supplied us with lodging, fire, food, clothes, and means of transport." "What people was it?" asked another. "The Dutch." "Ah, no people are more humane, though they are surrounded with savage nations."

Erasmus himself, for all his cosmopolitanism, was essentially Dutch in his aversion to violence, his love of peace and compromise, and his contempt of passion as a substitute for argument. These traits were part of his inheritance from the Brethren of the Common Life. For it was there that he received his early training. And when he came to Paris and entered the College of Montaigu, a university dormitory for poor students, he found himself in a familiar atmosphere. For the Regent of Montaigu, Johannes Standonck, son of a poor Mechelen cobbler, had studied with the Brethren of the Common Life at Gouda, and was assisted in the work he was doing in France by members of the Windesheim congregation.

Erasmus was not a theologian but a man of letters. His professed purpose in life was "to accustom literature, which among the Italians thus far had been almost pagan, to speaking of Christ." He had no sympathy with Luther's dogmatic scruples. He was concerned with the conduct of life, not with the niceties of doctrine. A heretic who lived decently and devoutly was, in his eyes, a better Christian than an orthodox sinner who went to confession regularly. It has been said of him that he laid the egg that was hatched by Luther. But it is more accurate to say that his word was the most eloquent expression of that concept of the Christian way of life which, thanks to the teaching of the Modern Devotion, was the common property of the inarticulate Dutch masses. That concept was not, in itself, heretical or hostile to the Church of Rome; but the devout saw its denial exemplified in the lives of so many prelates, priests, and friars that their ideal seemed less safe within than outside of its fold.

On June 16, 1520 the bull appeared whereby Pope Leo X condemned Luther's teaching as heresy. Jerome Aleander was sent as legate to the Netherlands in order to win the young emperor's support for the theses contained in the papal ban. His chances of success seemed slight. It was reported to him that at Bruges, on a recent visit, Charles V had been in the company of Erasmus, Thomas Morus, Vives, Hutten, and Peutinger, all of them men who were of a mind with the Dutch humanist. Aleander was received in audience at Antwerp. It was customary, on such occasions, for the Count of Chièvres to reply, after a whispered consultation with the emperor. But this time, to everyone's surprise, Charles answered himself, and declared his willingness to support the pope. He had inherited from his Burgundian forebears a policy of anti-French intrigue. He was anxious to gain papal aid against the traditional enemy of the Burgundian house. Purely political motives based on dynastic considerations made him side with Rome against Luther. That same evening he signed an edict ordering the destruction of Luther's books in all his lands. On October 8, 1520 the burghers of Louvain witnessed the first burning of his books in the market place. Erasmus, who was teaching there at the time, left the city a year later. And on April 23, 1522 François van der Hulst took office as inquisitor. That was the beginning of an era of merciless persecution, which was to end in open revolt by the terrorized masses and in the ultimate liberation of the Dutch from submission to a foreign dynasty.

CHAPTER III

Social Ferment

CHARLES V summoned delegates from all the Low Countries, not from his patrimonial provinces alone, to an assembly at Brussels on October 25, 1555. That not one province was excluded had its special reason. The sovereign wanted the representatives of all his Netherlands to be witnesses to his abdication and to the transfer of the reins of government to his son Philip.

Sir John Mason, who witnessed the scene as envoy of the court in London, wrote home that there was not one man in the assembly who did not weep copiously during the larger part of the monarch's address. Philip, speaking Spanish, expressed his regret that he could not speak either French or Flemish, and therefore requested Anthony Perrenot, Bishop of Arras, to speak on his behalf.

Thus, at the very outset of his reign, the new monarch gave public evidence of his estrangement from his Dutch subjects. The father was a native of the Flemish city of Ghent and familiar with the Dutch language. The son was a Spaniard in speech, in manners, and in feeling, and had nothing in common with the people of the Netherlands.

Yet he had every reason to cultivate their favor and affection. For the Low Countries were the most prosperous and the richest of all his dominions. Even the gold mines of Mexico and Peru yielded no more than one-fourth of the revenue that the Netherlands contributed to the king's exchequer. They paid, in fact, two millions of gold annually, which was four times as much as the combined receipts from Spain and the Indies.

The mainspring of this wealth was the industry of the people, in conjunction with the fertility of the land and its favorable site at the mouths of three great arteries of trade. Antwerp, at this time, had risen to first rank among its cities, while the proud cities of Flanders, Ghent, Bruges, and Ypres were in decline. Two causes had concurred in impairing their prosperity: the rivalry of the English cloth industry, which had been built up with the help of Flemish immigrants, and competition of rural looms. The cities had vainly sought to defend themselves against these interlopers by tightening the grip of the medieval guilds upon the industry. But their restrictions and protective devices were no longer suited to the spirit of the new age. Antwerp opened its port to the English cloth merchants, who made it the staple for the sale of their product on the Continent, and the Emperor Maximilian, who resentfully remembered the opposition of Ghent and Bruges against himself and his wife, went out of his way to favor and protect Antwerp's growth. He attracted foreigners to the young metropolis with liberal privileges. Whereas in Ghent and Bruges the foreigners found themselves hampered by all sorts of restrictive ordinances and regulations, they enjoyed perfect freedom in Antwerp, and equal rights with the natives. Instead of the medieval guild halls, where the manufactures offered for sale were under strict control of the municipal government, Antwerp had a modern exchange, where no wares were officially guaranteed and the slogan that was valid for all transactions was the Roman rule of *caveat emptor,* let the buyer beware.

A strange feature of this Antwerp commerce was the subordinate part that the citizens themselves played on this busy scene. The city's international trade was controlled by Italians, Spaniards, Portuguese, Englishmen, Scandinavians, and Germans. The Antwerp people benefited, of course, by the traffic these foreign interests brought to the city. But they were not among the leading merchants and shipowners. Most of the freight unloaded on the quays was brought to Antwerp in foreign vessels, and the provinces of Holland and Zeeland supplied the larger part of that carrying fleet.

Seafaring was one of the chief occupations of the inhabitants of these two counties. The ocean, of course, had supplied the coast dwellers with seafood since the beginnings of human life in those parts. In the Middle Ages the most popular of all fish was the herring. An early tradition, not very well authenticated, attributes to Jan Beukelszoon, a citizen of Biervliet, the invention of a process for preserving herring which made the fish a durable article of export. The technique was, no doubt, the outcome of the accumulated experience of generations of packers. The surplus catch for which there was no immediate consumption ceased to be a problem. The herring could henceforth be salted, barreled, and stored, or shipped to foreign parts to capture new markets.

This packing industry led to the rise of Dutch saltworks and a lively carrying trade to the coasts of France and the Canary Islands. For it was from there that the Hollanders obtained the needed salt; and the surplus not required by the packers or for home consumption was exported to the Baltic Sea together with Dutch dairy products, home-brewed beer, Leyden cloth, wines from France, and products from Mediterranean countries. The ships, on their return trips from the Baltic, brought timber, iron ore, copper, grain, and raw materials for various Dutch industries which, working for foreign markets, supplied the Dutch merchant fleet with an abundance of cargo. The towns on the Zuider Zee—Hoorn, Enkhuizen, Kampen, Zwolle, Amsterdam—were members of the German hansa, and had, as such, old connections with the ports along the Baltic, which were useful to them in the extension of this carrying trade.

The Dutch are thrifty by nature, and the influence of the Modern Devotion preserved them from recklessly squandering this new-won wealth. Their prosperity found expression in the comfort and furnishings of their homes. These were the object of foreign admiration and wonder. "To enter their houses," said Guicciardini, an Italian resident of Antwerp who published in 1566 an excellent "Description of the Low Countries," "and to behold the abundance of furniture and all sorts of household implements, all equally neat and exquisite, gives one much pleasure and even greater surprise, for there is, probably, nothing in the world that equals it." And Erasmus wrote in his *Adagia* that "merchants who have traveled across more than half the world admit that there is only one Holland as regards neatness of furniture."

One need not rely exclusively on the testimony of these writers. The painters of the fifteenth century have left us scenes of Dutch interiors that fully confirm it. Jan van Eyck's magnificent painting of John Arnolfini's living room at Bruges is one example among many. It dates from around 1435. It is the custom to speak of Van Eyck and his contemporaries as primitives, but that name does not define their highly developed style; it only reveals our ignorance of the tradition from which it derived. Their work was the full blossoming of a long growth.

Van Eyck came from the neighborhood of Maastricht, which was a famous art center as far back as the late twelfth century. Wolfram von Eschenbach wrote of his hero Parsifal: "As he sat on his horse, he was a picture such as no painter of Cologne or Maastricht could have painted better." Van Eyck, therefore, did not miraculously come out of a vacuum. He had a long tradition behind him, which was fostered by each successive generation until it reached fullness of expression in his paintings.

The same is true, of course, of all Dutch art. The amazing

concentration of so much talent in that small corner of the continent was no accident but the result of favorable conditions. The towns of the Low Countries, in the late Middle Ages, were busy centers of industrial activity. Weavers, clothmakers, dyers, potters, woodcarvers, sculptors, painters, blacksmiths—all plied their tools in workshops, yards, and studios. The artists belong in this group of handicraftsmen. One does not wrong the painters and sculptors by mentioning them in the same breath with potters, weavers, and blacksmiths. They were craftsmen pure and simple, and the potters and weavers and shipbuilders were artists in their crafts, each turning out a product that bore the stamp of his individual taste and of his love for the work of his hands.

The skill of these workers was the fruit of the accumulated experience of successive generations. The son grew up in his father's workshop and inherited with the shop the old man's technique. Apprentices came to the Low Countries from all parts of Europe, attracted by the fame of Dutch workmanship. They brought not only their energy but also new ideas that tended to improve traditional techniques and stimulate the growth of new ones. Albrecht Dürer's father was one of these. He came to the Netherlands from his native Hungary to work as an apprentice in a goldsmith's shop before he settled for good in Nürnberg. These itinerant craftsmen helped to spread among foreigners the fame of Dutch arts and crafts. As a consequence, buyers and collectors came to the Netherlands to purchase pictures and prints. Antwerp in the early sixteenth century was one of the great art markets of Europe.

The dukes of Burgundy were generous patrons of art. Jan van Eyck was first employed by John of Bavaria at The Hague, but after the latter's death he passed into the service of Philip the Good, whom he served not only as court painter but also on diplomatic missions. The court's patronage of art made it fashionable for noblemen and wealthy burghers to employ painters in imitation of the duke. Orders for altar pieces and portraits kept many a master busy in the cities of Flanders and Brabant, and attracted others from Holland and the Rhine province. Dirc Bouts left his native Haarlem and settled in Louvain; Gerard David, of Oudewater in Holland, and the German Hans Memlinc set up studios at Bruges. But although the southern Netherlands, on account of their closer proximity to France, were the center of art production in the Burgundian era, Holland in the north was not devoid of skillful masters. Haarlem is said to have been the cradle of Dutch landscape painting, and Dirc Bouts, who was born there, was the first to use views of gardens as backgrounds. Geertgen tot St. Jans, one of the great masters of that age, also worked at Haarlem toward the end of the fifteenth century. The next generation produced Lucas van Leyden (1494–1533). Others were at work at Amsterdam, Delft, Utrecht.

From the duchy of Brabant came two of the greatest and most original masters. Jerome Bosch (c. 1462–1516) of Bois-le-Duc was an eccentric, revolutionary genius who, instead of the faithful realism that is typical of the Dutch school, painted nightmarish visions and scenes of hell that look like modern, surrealistic creations of the subconscious. The other was Peter Brueghel the Elder. He was a lonely pioneer and his art a reaction against the style and the standards of his time. During the reign of Charles V the imitation of Italian art had come into vogue in the Netherlands. Jan Gossaert, called Mabuse, court painter of Philip, Bishop of Utrecht, had set the fashion, and the sensational success of that great master spurred lesser talents on to emulate his style. They were encouraged by the growing demand from Spain for pictures in the Italian manner. Brueghel's art was a reaction of native realism against this foreign influence, an esthetic revolt that coincided with the people's revolt against Spanish rule. He drove the nude heroes of classical mythology off the canvas and in their stead painted the native crowd with naked realism.

Brueghel's art was not only an esthetic but also a social protest. Disfigured shapes, hunchbacks, cripples, blind beggars, drunkards, idiots, epileptics, legless grotesques, all the wreckage of a time that was out of joint, were rendered by him with poignant realism. The pain and the pity that stirred within him at the spectacle of their ugliness found expression in the beauty of their portrayal. His own features had nothing in common with the types that he preferred to paint. A finely cut profile, a high forehead, and a dreamy expression are the striking traits of that noble face. By the testimony of that portrait—a contemporary copperplate—Peter Brueghel, though of peasant stock, was akin to the great visionaries and thinkers of the Reformation period, himself a reformer both of social and artistic consciousness.

The dukes of Burgundy were also patrons of music. The period from about 1450 to 1550 has been called the golden age in the history of that art, and much of its music is the work of Netherlands composers. "Here are the true masters of music, who have restored and perfected that art," wrote Guicciardini, "for it is so native to them that men and women sing naturally to measure, with great charm and melody. And having joined art to nature, they make such demonstration and harmony with voices and all sorts of instruments as every one can see and hear and may be found in all the courts of Christian princes." He adds a list of their names, twenty-seven in all, including Josken de Prez, Obrecht, Okeghem, Orlando Lasso. Yet the list is not exhaustive, for he concludes it by saying, "and many other talented maestros, who are very famous and scattered all over the world in honorable positions and high stations."

Art and music speak a language that is universally understood. Painters and composers were welcome visitors wherever they went, and native wanderlust impelled many a young artist to seek employment and fame in foreign lands. Roger van der Weyden was in Rome in 1450 and worked for the Duchess of Milan and for Lionello d'Este in Ferrara. Jan van Scorel, of Haarlem, went to the Holy Land, and passed through Italy on the way home. Anton Mor, a native of Utrecht, became court painter of Charles V at Madrid. The musicians had even stronger motives for travel in search of foreign patronage. The painters who stayed at home could sell their works at local fairs or at the art markets of Antwerp and other Dutch cities. There was no market for musical compositions. Composers made a living as choirmaster or organist, and the number of private chapels whose owners could afford to maintain a concertmaster was limited in the Netherlands. Hence these talented masters of whom Guicciardini wrote scattered to the four winds to make music and compose for foreign patrons.

Literature, on the other hand, had no range beyond the native scene. No other art is so exclusively national and so inaccessible to the outsider. It is a people's communing with itself. And since the Burgundian dukes were not of the people, but foreigners unacquainted with the language, Dutch poetry was slighted or ignored, a poor Cinderella who sat by the fireside while her sisters, Music and Art, were being feted at court.

Since the court ignored her, the cultured despised her. As a result, she was not cared for or trained to speak the language of the cultured. The literary output of the Burgundian era is poor compared to that of Maerlant's age. There are a number of short secular dramas of the late fourteenth century that have a naïve, artless charm. There are a couple of Brussels mystery plays that bear comparison with similar plays in French and English. And there are, best of all, two little dramas of the late fifteenth century that must have impressed a larger group than the national audience. For both were translated into contemporary English. One is *Mary of*

Nimmegen, a sort of female Faustus, the other the morality of *Elckerlijc,* the original of *Everyman.* If it were not for these high spots and the prose writings of the mystics, the landscape of Dutch literature would be a flat and uninspiring scene indeed.

Plenty of verse was being written, but to the burghers who were its begetters the writing of it was not an emotional necessity but merely a social sport. They came together in what they called Chambers of Rhetoric, a kind of theater guilds which, like the labor guilds, had their origin in church organizations. These Chambers were an essential feature of urban life in the fifteenth and sixteenth centuries. Nearly every town of any importance had its Chamber, and vied with its neighbors in dramatic composition and stagecraft. One town would act as host to the others and arrange within its walls a competition between their Chambers. Each would enter the town with flying banners, gay costumes, and the accompaniment of music, and show its play to an audience composed of citizens from all the competing towns and the surrounding country. Prizes were awarded for the best costumes, the best acting, and the best play.

The Dutch had a curious name for such a festival. They called it *Landjuweel,* that is, Land Jewel. They were an occasion for extravagant display, as no town would be outshone by any neighbor in wealth and magnificence. But the verse was seldom on a par with the splendor of the show. Many plays were written in sheer doggerel, to which the makers had done their best to give resonance and beauty by an abundant use of French bastard words. As specimens of literature these plays have little value; they are precious, however, as mirrors of the life and manners of the age.

The government of Charles V did not always look with favor on these Land Jewel shows. When Protestantism began to spread its teaching, the new doctrine found a sounding board in the stage of the Chambers of Rhetoric. The plays were an outlet for popular grievances, and an heretical *Factor* (the leading poet of the Chamber whose task it was to write its plays) had the dangerous opportunity to broadcast his misguided notions through the mouths of the actors. The burgher stage became a rival of the pulpit and a threat to the authorities.

The new art of printing helped to spread the new doctrines. Books made a deeper and more lasting impression than the ephemeral word that was heard from the stage. They were treasured and reread in the intimacy of the home, discussed and handed around among friends. The masses were not illiterate. The Modern Devotion had fostered respect and care for a good education. We have Guicciardini's word for it that "the larger part of the people have some rudiments of grammar; at any rate, nearly all, down to the peasants, can read and write." Hence the printing presses in the Netherlands had their share in spreading the Reformed religion. They catered chiefly to the learned and the burgher classes, supplying the former with Latin books, the latter with devotional tracts in the vernacular. The nobility read French. Besides, to buy printed books was not yet fashionable among high society. Margaret of Savoy, who was the emperor's first governess in the Netherlands, possessed a rich library in her palace at Mechelen, but it contained only French manuscripts and no printed books except one in Italian, as we know from the inventory of her collection that she wrote with her own hand in the year 1516. Yet several presses, by that time, had been turning out books in the Netherlands for half a century. Printers were active in Gouda, Delft, Leyden, Haarlem, Utrecht, Deventer, Antwerp; and many others, in the track of musicians and painters, wandered away and set up presses abroad, in England, Germany and Italy.

The conditions on the land did not present so pleasant a picture of many-sided industry and prosperity. They were better, it is true, than they had been before the Burgundian era. The peasant was no longer a serf of the little tyrant of his fields. The *keurmede,* an ancient right that gave the lord of the manor first claim to what he considered the choicest piece in the movable estate of a deceased serf, was, perhaps, the last vestige of feudalism that lingered on in the more backward regions. The peasant was virtually a free man, and tilled the land either as freeholder or as a tenant of the absent owner, be it a church, a convent, a wealthy burgher, a nobleman, or, if the fields were part of the domain, the county.

The nobility was no longer the predominant landowning class. Guicciardini says that instead of investing their surplus cash in improvement of their arable land and livestock, they had begun to give it in deposit at Antwerp in the hope of making twelve per cent interest, and more, with the result that much land was going to waste and the rural laboring class was impoverished for lack of employment. Declining yields from their deteriorated lands and unsuccessful speculation forced many noblemen to dispose of their property. The Dutch historian Montanus, writing half a century after Guicciardini, ascribed the cause of the nobility's decline to the loss of landed estates which they sold to the clergy and wealthy burghers.

In the county of Holland the rural population was still backward and poor. The feuds between the Hooks and the Cods had been calamitous for the peasants. Their lands had been damaged by fighting forces, their cattle stolen, their homes plundered. Repeated inroads of the sea caused periodic ruin and despair. General poverty prevailed in the watery region north of the IJ. In the early nineties of the fifteenth century the peasants there revolted against the Burgundian administration. They wore, as a token of their penury, a lump of bread and cheese on their chests, and from this badge they got the name of Bread-and-Cheese Rabble.

Tax gatherers and law officers were the chief victims of their wrath. But their ill-disciplined and badly armed bands were no match for the troops of the Burgundian governor. They were beaten, forced to pay the hated levies and back taxes and heavy penalties besides to atone for their insurrection. The rule of the foreigner was generally hated in those rural parts, and disobedience to the orders of his administration was almost a matter of principle. When the young emperor, at that fatal audience in Antwerp, endorsed the papal ban on all heresies, his action had no deterrent effect upon these people. On the contrary, it gave fresh impetus to the defection from the Church of Rome.

They were not followers of Luther. He was admired among them for his heroic defiance of Rome, but Lutheranism was never popular in the Netherlands. The Brethren of the Common Life had stressed the value of good works; Luther, on the other hand, taught that there was no justification except through faith. Luther's tracts were circulated in translation, but only those devotional writings in which the specifically Lutheran point of view was not apparent. The Dutch version of Luther's German Bible was far from a faithful rendering. The translator had taken great liberties with the original text, making changes in the Reformer's commentaries, omitting passages, and occasionally even contradicting him. Luther had written contemptuously of the Epistle of James, in which it is said, "What doth it profit, my brethren, though a man say he hath faith, and have not works? Can faith save him?" Not one of the many editions of the Dutch Bible contains Luther's condemnation of that passage. Luther had called it "an Epistle of straw." But the Dutch people, imbued with the spirit of the Modern Devotion, saw in it an expression of their own belief. They were indebted to Luther for having proclaimed the sole authority of the Scriptures, and followed his teaching in refusing to follow his authority as against the Scriptures in this matter of justification through faith alone.

The teachings of the Anabaptists, on the other hand, appealed to the masses. To them the Bible was the only code of law they recognized, and brotherly love the bond that held society together. The poor in spirit, the victims of social injustice, the radical thinkers, the unbalanced, the extremists, found comfort in so simple a gospel. It came out of Germany, but had its strongest following in Holland. Jan Mathysen, of Haarlem, founded in 1534 the New Jerusalem at Münster in Westphalia. The faithful were ordered to repair to this kingdom of God upon earth. Disobedience to the summons meant eternal damnation. Thousands in Holland left their homes, were caught on the way by armed forces of the authorities, and thrown into prison. After Mathysen had fallen in battle, Jan Beukelszoon of Leyden reigned as King of the New Jerusalem. The overthrow of this fanatic demagogue, in whom the faithful actually believed as a savior, had a wholesome reaction. Under the leadership of Menno Simons, of Franeker in Friesland, the Anabaptists were weaned away from past excesses and organized into a quiet, undogmatic sect, withdrawn from the world and chiefly concerned with the search for the straight and narrow path that leads to God. But the memory of the Münster atrocities made them suspect long after they had become a meek and harmless community. The martyrs of the first decades of the Reformation in the Netherlands were mostly followers of Menno. They died, strong in their faith, with heroic resignation. Their confessions and last letters, collected and published in 1562, are a moving testimony to their sincerity and piety.

But these simple unworldly souls did not possess the mettle that is needed to resist injustice and rebel against tyrannic authorities. The strength that dared defy the Spanish sovereign came from another, more militant, faith, the doctrine of Calvin. Calvinism had armed itself with a clearly defined concept of state and society. It insisted on discipline and solid organization. It inspired fervor and zeal, rather than meekness and resignation in its followers. Theirs was not the spirit of the Sermon on the Mount but the self-assurance of the Old Testament Hebrews.

In the fifties and sixties Calvinism began its conquest of the Low Countries, first of the French-speaking border regions in the south, from which it spread rapidly, through Brabant and Flanders, into the northern provinces. Mennonism lingered on, but as a humble, inactive sect of the inarticulate layers of society. The long-smoldering discontent among all classes, fed by administrative reforms, heavy taxation, abuses in the church, the terror of the Inquisition, was fanned into flame by the wind of religious fervor that blew northward from Huguenot France. The Reformatory movements from Germany had run their course. It was from France that the Netherlands received the doctrine that they could wholeheartedly embrace. Charles V had sided with Rome against Luther to gain papal support against France, and the persecution of his heretical subjects to which that ill-advised choice compelled him resulted in the spiritual conquest of the Netherlands by French Calvinism.

CHAPTER IV

Revolt

KING PHILIP II inherited with his father's dominions the ancient rivalry of the Burgundians with the King of France. Charles had been at war with the latter since 1542, and he handed to his son, among many other burdens, the task of making a satisfactory peace with the enemy. The war was not popular in the Netherlands, for it was being waged for no other purpose than to secure for Spain a firm foothold in Italy. Philip finally succeeded in concluding an advantageous treaty at Cateau-Cambrésis which left Spain supreme in Italy, and soon afterward he left the Low Countries for Madrid, never to return.

Before his departure the States-General of the patrimonial provinces met at Ghent and made demands that sorely offended his pride. They refused to grant him his *bede* unless they were allowed to administer the levies through their own commissioners, and successfully insisted on the withdrawal of the Spanish forces, three thousand men in all, whom the king wanted to leave garrisoned in the Netherlands.

An ominous sign of the oncoming storm was the attitude of the high nobility. Most of them were Knights of the Golden Fleece and supposed to be devoted to the service of the monarch who was its commander. They were, as such, members of the Council of State, but had little say in government affairs, since all important matters were decided by the Privy Council, which received its orders direct from the monarch. They were made to share responsibility for those decisions without having a voice in framing them. They realized that the prestige of their names was used to inspire in the people a false confidence in the good intentions of the absolute ruler. To serve merely as window dressing was galling to their pride and self-respect.

First among these nobles was William, Prince of Orange. He was not a Netherlander. The language that came readiest to his tongue was French, still he was not a Frenchman either, though he bore the title of Prince of Orange. He was born a German as eldest son of a Count of Nassau, and spent his childhood in the ancestral castle of Dillenburg on the Dill, a tributary of the Lahn. An older brother of his father was head of the Netherlands branch of the Nassaus which had owned extensive possessions in the Low Countries ever since the early fifteenth century. But this branch became extinct in 1544 by the death of Count René, who from his mother's family had inherited the princedom of Orange, in the south of France. Under his will René had appointed his eldest cousin, Count William of Nassau-Dillenburg, sole heir to his rich possessions in the Netherlands and France.

William was then a boy of eleven. His mother had brought him up in the Lutheran religion. Would the emperor allow the young heretic to succeed to his cousin's rich estate? The emperor did give his consent, but on conditions that were calculated to estrange him from his home and native land. The father had to waive all claims to the guardianship of his eldest son, the boy was to live in the Netherlands, and would receive a Roman Catholic education consonant with the high rank he was destined to hold among the Netherlands nobility and at the Burgundian court in Brussels.

He soon became a favorite of the emperor. Vivacity, great self-control, and an affable manner ingratiated him with high and low. These gifts and his great wealth and princely rank made him one of the most popular courtiers, but amid flattery, temptation, and riotous living, he kept a steady head and his moral balance. At the age of twenty, he was given a captaincy and served with his company in a campaign against France. In October, 1555, he was called to Brussels to attend the assembly of the States-General in which Charles V abdicated. Leaning on the shoulder of the young Prince of Orange, the monarch made his farewell address.

"In the multitude of words there wanteth not sin; but he that refraineth his lips is wise," says the Book of Proverbs. But the Prince of Orange's taciturnity was not a virtue in the opinion of those who first called him the Silent. They meant to imply by the name that he was a secretive hypocrite, the type of diplomat that uses words to conceal his meaning. He was, indeed, past master of that art. He himself has told the story of an incident that illustrates his diplomatic skill. In 1559 he was sent to Paris, together with the Duke of Alva, as a hostage for the execution of the peace treaty of Cateau-Cambrésis. One day, King Henry II and the prince rode together through the Bois de Vincennes. The king, who thought that the prince enjoyed King Philip's full confidence, began to talk about a wicked scheme of which Prince William knew nothing. The two monarchs were planning to help each other in wiping out all heresies among their subjects and restore the Catholic religion to sole power through a general massacre of Protestants. The prince said no word that could betray his ignorance of this hellish plot. He let the king talk on until he knew all the evil that was brewing. And it was then and there that he resolved to do his utmost to save his Netherlands compatriots from the fate that his royal master planned to inflict on them.

When King Philip left the Netherlands for good in 1559, he had no illusions as to the prince's feelings toward him. The latter saw his royal master off at Flushing, and in the course of the conversation said something in mitigation of the seditious attitude of the States-General. The king flared up at those words and, in hot anger, retorted, "Not the

States, but you, you, you!" It is an anecdote that crops up at a much later date, but though it may not be authentic in substance, it is a true reflection of the tense relationship between the two men.

The prince, at that time, had not yet thrown in his lot with the people, but Philip knew quite well to which side his sympathies went. One of his instructions to the prince in parting was to order the arrest of a number of well-to-do citizens in his Stadtholderate of Holland and Zeeland, and to have them tried on a charge of heresy. Prince William had the intended victims of the king's wrath secretly warned; and when his officers moved to make the arrests, the birds had flown.

Tens of thousands fled the country in this way with the connivance of the native authorities. They found a refuge in Emden, in Wesel, in Cologne, in London, and the seaports of the south of England. The organization of the exiles into a church was started at Emden. This became the cradle of the Dutch Reformed Church, which was to create cohesion and discipline among the dispersed and give leadership to the rising masses in the homeland. Its first synod met at Wesel in 1568 and provisionally adopted Calvin's Presbyterian polity. Three years later the synod of Emden confirmed this action. The participants agreed on a confession of faith as a formula of their unity. The name Consistory was adopted for the board—the minister, elders and deacons—of each church, and provision made for their meeting once a week. Ministers were to be called by the Consistory subject to the approval of the Classis, an assembly of delegates from the several churches within a given area. The Heidelberg catechism was adopted, and a Dutch version of the psalms. Thus Calvinism organized the Reformed into a democratic and defiant church prepared to challenge the powers of Rome and of the Spanish Inquisition.

The Reformation had found many supporters among the

nobility. Some were sincere converts, but there were others who joined the opposition against the administration in resentment at the growing power of the *noblesse de robe*. They were hostile to the king out of hatred for his absolutism, and when they saw that his claim to absolute authority, under the pope, in matters of faith met with bitter resistance among all classes of society, they threw all caution to the wind and made common cause with the Reformed.

Their first attack was upon Antoine Perrenot, Lord of Granvelle. He was the right-hand man of Margaret, Duchess of Parma, a stepsister of King Philip, who had made her his regent in the Netherlands. Granvelle had been appointed archbishop of Mechelen when the new ecclesiastical organization was introduced in 1559. Two years later he had been created cardinal. These preferments, and the unmistakable evidence of his hold on the administration, made him generally suspected, though unjustly, as the prime mover of the hated church reform and the intensified heresy hunt that ensued. The Knights of the Golden Fleece in the Council of State repeatedly demanded his recall. The king was loath to let his trustiest and ablest counselor go, but if he maintained him in power, he would lose the loyalty and confidence of the highest nobility of the Netherlands. He chose at last the lesser loss, and recalled the cardinal in 1564.

The lower nobility came into action the following year. They concluded a league, which they called Compromise, for the redress of grievances and the cessation of the heresy hunt. Its leaders were the brothers John and Philip van Marnix, both fervent Calvinists; but many malcontents of the Catholic faith made common cause with them. The Prince of Orange remained aloof, but his brother Louis, Count of Nassau, an ardent Protestant, kept him informed of all that happened inside the league.

In April, 1566, a deputation of the League, about three hundred men strong, went to call on the Duchess of Parma at Brussels and handed her a petition for abrogation of the Inquisition and the edicts against the heretics. The duchess was helpless. In a meeting with members of the Council of State, the Privy Council, and the Knights of the Golden Fleece, where the impending petition had been discussed, she had heard the Knights express their approval of its contents. She dared not oppose them, but neither had she the courage to defy the king by consenting to the desired repeal. She chose a middle way, by promising to send the petition to His Majesty and give orders to the inquisitors to proceed with moderation for the time being.

An early tradition traces to this occasion the origin of the name *Geus,* which the rebels adopted as a term of honor. The Seigneur de Berlaymont, one of the Duchess Margaret's counselors, is said to have reassured the frightened woman with the words, "Comment, Madame, votre Altesse a-t-elle crainte de ces gueux?" (How now, Madame, is your Highness afraid of these beggars?) The question was overheard by the Lord of Brederode and at his suggestion the name *geus* was accepted by them as an earnest of their determination to remain loyal to the king unto beggary.

It was a feeble and transparent pretense that could deceive no one, least of all the king, who was suspicious by nature and too well informed by his sister and her counselors to take their protestation of loyalty at face value. The nobles themselves had no illusions on that score. The two from their midst who were chosen to present the petition to the king in person departed for Madrid with a heavy heart. Their misgivings were well founded. One died soon after his arrival, the other was thrown into prison from which only death was to release him.

But while their return was anxiously awaited, the sorely tried patience of the persecuted masses suddenly broke. Their pent-up fury burst into flame one summer day in 1566. In an access of mass madness mobs invaded churches and monasteries and struck the images of saints from their niches and pedestals in retaliation for so many victims of the Inquisition. The trouble started at Antwerp but rapidly spread throughout all the Low Countries. The rioters laid hands on precious and irreplaceable gifts from the pious of previous generations: paintings by the early Dutch masters, sculpture in stone and wood, stained-glass windows, gold and silver vessels, religious vestments. To the wreckers these treasures were not things of beauty but symbols of the heartless tyranny that had persecuted them.

The king's reply to this outrage was the mission of the Duke of Alva, the Iron Duke, as he was called. His very name struck terror into the hearts of the people. His arrival, at the head of his dreaded soldiery, hushed them into abject quiet and despair.

It was then that Prince William of Orange openly took the side of the Dutch against their Spanish sovereign. He had not condoned the sack of the churches. On the contrary, he had unequivocally condemned the iconoclasts and, as Burggrave of Antwerp, restored order there with severity. His native moderation hated all excesses. He hated tyranny, but he hated mob rule no less. And when he saw that the brief spasm of riotous fury was seized upon as a pretext for more cruel persecution, he left the Netherlands for Germany to raise an army with money partly his own and partly borrowed from German princes who favored the Protestant cause.

The assumption of leadership over an armed revolt against the sovereign was an extreme step to take. The prince did not take it, to be sure, until all other attempts to protect the Dutch people had failed. He was often accused by more impulsive contemporaries of hesitancy and procrastination. The entrance to the palace of the Nassaus at Brussels bore the Latin inscription *Tardando Progredior,* I progress by tarrying. William of Orange turned that device into practice. He did not rush headlong into the perilous adventure of the revolt. He realized that, before the die should be cast, all discontented elements had to agree on armed resistance as their only chance of salvation. In the years 1565 to 1567 matters had not yet developed so far. There was general resentment at Spanish tyranny and the persecution of heretics, but opinions were divided as to the people's right to revolt. Even among the Reformed there was no unanimity on that score. The Lutherans denied that right, and the prince, son of a pious Lutheran mother, though himself brought up as a Catholic, was no doubt influenced by Lutheran scruples, for he had been reconverted to the Lutheran faith in 1566.

The Walloon refugees in London counseled their countrymen at home against resort to violence. It was unlawful, they believed, to break open a prison in order to free condemned heretics. But they had no objection to the use of false keys. To carry arms was permissible as a means of frightening enemies, but the use of them could not be allowed. And among the Dutch Reformed refugees in London armed resistance was condemned as contrary to Christ's word to Peter: "Put up again thy sword into his place; for all they that take the sword shall perish with the sword."

Such opinions could not fail to have their effect upon those who had remained behind under the Spanish yoke. It would be hazardous to rebel without being able to count upon assistance of their own kith and kin from abroad. Besides, there was the authority of Calvin himself to dissuade the individual burgher from offering resistance to the oppressor. In his *Institutes of the Christian Religion,* which was published in Dutch in 1560, the great Reformer taught that the highest authorities in the state had no absolute power over its citizens, but shared their power with the magistracies. One had to keep the other in check, so as to maintain a proper balance. When that balance, however, was disturbed by the monarch's tyranny or despotism, the magistrates had not only the right but the duty to interfere and restore the proper equilibrium. Private citizens, however, had no such right. They had to suffer and obey. Only when the will of the tyrant should run directly counter to God's commandment were they free to refuse obedience. For according to Peter and the other apostles "one ought to obey God rather than men."

There were, however, more radical elements who, disregarding Bible texts and Calvin, wanted to resort to arms. A strong party among the Dutch nobility was of that mind, and Prince William's favorite brother Louis of Nassau, who belonged to the Reformed religion, was a leader among them. And the Reformed Consistory of the Church in Antwerp was the kernel of a war party recruited from among the citizenry. But they did not represent the great mass of the people, and not until the nation as a whole could be counted upon would the Prince of Orange take up arms against the sovereign.

In 1566, shortly after the iconoclastic riots, a united front of moderates and radicals, of nobility and citizenry, of Lutherans and Calvinists was actually accomplished. All parties agreed on a petition to the King of Spain for the grant of religious freedom, in return for which he was offered the payment of three million gold florins. How different a course the history of Europe would have taken if Philip II had consented to this deal!

The Duke of Alva soon felt himself master of the situation. He crushed with little effort two attempts of the Prince of Orange and his brothers to invade the country from Germany. He drove terror into the nobility by the execution of two of the greatest among them, the counts of Egmont and Hoorne, on the scaffold in the market place at Brussels. He silenced all murmurs of rebellion by sending thousands of heretics to their death and leaving their dependents destitute by the confiscation of their estates. Encouraged by the quiet into which the people were hushed by these first symptoms of frightfulness, he proceeded to levy imposts that had no precedent in the history of the Low Countries. Commerce was paralyzed, tens of thousands fled abroad, seeking refuge in the harbor towns of England and East Friesland, or on board the privateers that were scouring the Channel and North Sea.

The united front that the prince had tried to build up was suddenly scattered beyond hope of repair. The majority of the nobles, warned by the fate of Egmont and Hoorne, made their peace with the Duke of Alva and the King. The magistracies of the cities were stricken dumb with fear. What resistance could the Netherlands offer to the matchless power of the Spanish Empire? It seemed reckless folly to attempt it. And yet the Prince of Orange, in the midst of terror-stricken despair, dared the impossible and assumed the leadership of an armed revolt.

He was aided miraculously by the Duke of Alva. For his reign of terror defeated its own end. By leaving the people no glimmer of hope, they drew courage from their very despair. It needed only one signal success to stir them into action. A bold exploit of the Sea Beggars, a sixteenth-century commando raid, gave them hope and courage. These pirates carried letters of marque from the Prince of Orange, and on April 1, 1572, they seized the town of Brielle in his name and held it successfully against a Spanish relief force. This victory over the enemy dispelled the gloom and stirred a general spirit of revolt. Town after town renounced its allegiance to the King of Spain and proclaimed its trust in the Prince of Orange.

So sudden was this uprising that the Duke of Alva had to abandon, for the time being, his tax-gathering campaign, in order to reduce the seditious towns to obedience by force of arms. Towns that tried to resist, such as Zutphen, Naarden, and Haarlem, were sacked and the burghers put to death. But Alkmaar and Leyden were never taken, and their successful defiance of the tyrant stiffened the people's determination not to bow under his yoke.

The motives for their revolt were mixed. The old discontent over the centralizing tendencies of the Burgundian government was as bitter as ever. Local patriotism still clung to ancient customs, privileges, and laws that were a cherished survival of the past. The bewildering diversity of municipal and provincial administrations was a survival from medieval times, but since it was a native product the people preferred it to the modern improvements imported from Burgundy and Spain. Still, the Dutch might have resigned themselves to its loss if King Philip had not attempted to enforce uniformity also in matters of faith. Political modernism concluded for religion's sake an unholy alliance with the reactionary forces of the Inquisition, and the senseless cruelties inflicted upon heretics were more than the people could bear. They went to war for freedom of religion, yet if the conflict had been a religious struggle only, the Dutch Catholics would not have joined the anti-Spanish uprising. But Roman Catholics did fight side by side with the Reformed, for as Dutchmen they opposed an alien rule that menaced their political liberty.

For that reason the secular leaders of the rebellion were anxious to emphasize its political aspect and leave the cause of religion out of account. In Prince William's manifestoes chief stress was laid on the necessity for restoring the freedoms by destroying Alva's tyranny. If he proclaimed the cause to be a revolt not against Spanish rule alone but also against Rome, he might alienate the Catholics from the common cause. The zealous among the Reformed, on the other hand, would admit no other motive than religious fervor. In 1574, the municipal government of Leyden, then besieged by the Spanish, issued emergency paper money which bore the inscription *Haec Libertatis ergo,* This for liberty's sake.

The Reverend Taling disapproved of the legend and did not hesitate to say so from the pulpit. In a vigorous sermon he called the city rulers to task for proclaiming on the city's currency that the people were fighting for freedom. *Haec Religionis ergo*, should have been the inscription, he said. The burgomaster, Adriaan van der Werff, and his secretary, Jan van Hout, were sitting side by side in the magistrates' pew. Van Hout, a fiery young man, felt his blood boiling at the minister's arraignment of the authorities. He pulled a loaded pistol out of his belt and, turning to the burgomaster, asked, "Shall I bring him down?" but Van der Werff laid a hand on his arm and restrained the young hotspur from committing murder in church.

Leyden's heroic resistance under Burgomaster van der Werff was rewarded with the establishment of a university within its walls. The time did not seem auspicious for the opening of an academy. The province of Holland was the only one of the Low Countries that had succeeded in expelling the Spaniards. All the land to the east and south was in the enemies' hands, and her own metropolis, the city of Amsterdam, was still a stronghold of Spanish power. Would the Prince of Orange and his faithful Hollanders be able to hold their own? No one could answer that question. They put their trust in God and founded an academy in the city of Leyden at a time when the fields and pastures all around lay ruined by inundation and the havoc of war.

The charter that conferred upon Leyden the honor of receiving the new university bears the date of January 6, 1575. The city had been relieved from the besieging Spaniards on October 3, 1574. The plans for the new foundation were conceived and worked out in the short space of three months. The charter was issued in the name of Philip, by the grace of God King of Castile, Leon and Aragon, and sovereign Lord of the Netherlands. That was not done for a joke. The prince was in bitter earnest and not in the mood for staging a farce. He was the sovereign's stadtholder in the province of Holland and claimed that he was not a rebel against his sovereign but the champion of his sovereign's Dutch subjects against the king's misguided regent and his cruel soldiers. The charter represented King Philip as a compassionate prince who pitied his people's plight in their war-stricken country. It distressed him, he was made to say, to see Dutch children lagging behind their comrades of neighboring countries in the matter of education. For that reason, and because the burghers of Leyden had borne themselves so loyally during the siege, the king, after ripe deliberation and on the advice of his beloved cousin, the Prince of Orange, decided to establish a university at Leyden.

It was a strange, ironical document. In it the prince, with grim mockery, took the monarch at his own word. For when Philip assumed the reins of government he had sworn to rule the Netherlands according to their laws and to maintain their privileges; and in his letters to the Council of State he had repeatedly described himself as a patient and merciful prince and loving father of his children. In the Leyden charter the Prince of Orange made him play the part of the noble benefactor that he had promised, and shamefully failed, to be. The document was a subtle rebuke to a perjured sovereign.

Alva, meanwhile, had been recalled and replaced by Don Louis de Requesens. Since his terroristic rule had failed to restore order, Philip was inclined to try what moderation could accomplish. But the insurgents in Holland were no longer in the mood to be coaxed by a show of reasonableness. They had tasted the sweet fruits of success and were determined to pluck a richer crop. They were enjoying liberty and self-government. For in the summer of 1572, fully three months after the raid on Brielle, Dordrecht, as the oldest of the cities of Holland, had called a meeting of the States of that province in its ancient city hall. The nobility was represented by two of its members, eleven towns sent delegates, and Philip van Marnix was present as spokesman for the Prince of Orange. The assembly recognized the latter as stadtholder in spite of the fact that King Philip had deposed him, discussed measures of defense on land and sea, swore to the prince, and received from him a solemn oath of faith, guaranteed freedom of religion to both Calvinists and Catholics until the States-General should decide otherwise, and voted generous appropriations for the upkeep of the prince's army.

The tolerance shown to the Catholics was of brief duration. A year later the observance of the Catholic religion was forbidden by the same deputies who at Dordrecht had voted to respect its freedom. The real estate of the church in the province was confiscated and used for the maintenance of Calvinist churches, and Catholics were excluded as a rule—though not a hard and fast one—from participation in both municipal and provincial government.

This about-face was due, no doubt, to the indignation created among the Reformed by the massacre of the French Huguenots on St. Bartholomew's Day, August 24, 1572. The Catholics could not be trusted, was the feeling aroused by the news of this outrage. The blow struck at the Calvinist religion in France jeopardized also the cause of the Dutch insurgents. Prince William had been hoping that King Charles IX would declare war on Spain and thus relieve Spanish pressure on the Low Countries. But after the murder of the Huguenot leaders he could no longer expect any aid from France. The un-co-operative attitude of certain Catholic elements in the municipal councils of Haarlem and other cities seemed to justify the antipopish attitude of the zealous.

Among the recalcitrant cities which, under Catholic control, still refused to support the prince, Amsterdam was first and foremost. The possession of great wealth makes its owners halfhearted. They want to keep things going on as they are. Every change meets with opposition from their side as a dangerous scheme of radicalism that spells the end of civilization. The rich merchants who ruled Amsterdam were no exception to this rule. For the sake of their profitable seaborne commerce they maintained the city's allegiance to the King of Spain. The ships of a rebel port could expect no mercy from the Spanish men-of-war. Loyalty to the sovereign meant lasting prosperity; loyalty to the prince's cause meant financial ruin. But the common people of Amsterdam, the majority of whom had embraced the Reformed religion, were not satisfied with a cowardly policy dictated by the money interests. Headed by agents of the Prince of Orange they seized the pro-Spanish magistracy and shipped them outside the city walls. It was a good-natured, bloodless rebellion, but none the less effective. For from that year on—it happened in 1578—Amsterdam supported steadfastly, with money, ships, and man power, the Prince of Orange's fight for freedom.

The prince was not to see its victorious conclusion. When he died at the hands of an assassin on July 10, 1584, he could not foresee the triumph of the cause that he had championed at the price of his fortune and his life. His dying words, "My God, have mercy upon me and this poor people!" expressed no confidence in the victory of right over might. The twelve years that elapsed between the capture of Brielle and his murder in Delft form a record of discomfitures rarely relieved by good fortune and success. A fatal weakness of the Dutch was their lack of national unity. Local and provincial selfishness found it difficult to yield to the good of the common cause. The Dutch people renounced their medieval past in seceding from the Church of Rome; they sought to perpetuate it in seceding from the Spanish Empire. But this very aversion to a centralized government that helped to stimulate their revolt imperiled its chances of success. For it sorely hampered the prince's endeavors to consolidate the various provinces for united action. In 1579 his brother John of Nassau brought about the Union of Utrecht, which became the cornerstone of the Dutch Republic. It was not the best that he desired, but the next best that he could obtain. It was a makeshift agreement arrived at under the pressure of imminent danger by a few of the northern provinces despairing at the moment of joint resistance of all the Netherlands against the Spanish armies. A free confederacy of all the Low Countries was the ultimate aim that the Prince of Orange had in view, but he never saw it consummated. There did exist on parchment a union of all the provinces, the so-called Pacification of Ghent of 1576, and the constituents of the Union of Utrecht took good care to state that it was not their intention to withdraw from that general federation. But the union of north and south for which the Pacification made provision was never realized in fact. The south—that is, those provinces now constituting the kingdom of Belgium—gave up the struggle a decade later, and submitted to the power of Spain; the north alone persisted and fought its way through to freedom and autonomy. But when Prince William closed his eyes, even that partial triumph was still uncertain.

Still, the triumph was his, thanks to the living thought that he bequeathed to his people and the world. Through the word and through the thought it embodied he was to conquer. The Prince of Orange was a master in the art of bringing the word which carried his counsel to the people at home and abroad. With the help of great scholars and writers he conducted an able press campaign which pleaded the cause of the Netherlands against the King of Spain before the bar of European public opinion. He put his trust not in force but in the intangible power of that opinion, which could not fail to be impressed by the brave struggle of a helpless people against a mighty empire.

In 1580 King Philip issued an edict proscribing the prince as "chief perturber and corrupter of entire Christianity and especially of the Netherlands," and calling on all and everyone "to free us of this pest and deliver him dead or alive," the reward being a sum of twenty-five thousand crowns in gold or in estates, full pardon for any crime committed, and a patent of nobility. The prince's answer to this ignoble document was a fiery *Apology* in which he reviewed his life and the part he had played in the Netherlands, refuting point for point the accusations leveled against him in the ban. He disclaimed the charge that he was a rebel and traitor, for as the heir to the princedom of Orange, which he held in absolute sovereignty, he was the equal, not the subject, of the sovereign ruler of the Netherlands. "The mischief," he wrote, "has all arisen from the cruelty and arrogance of the Spaniard, who thinks he can make slaves of us, as if we were Indians or Italians; of us who have never been a conquered people, but have accepted a ruler under definite conditions. This is the cancer that we have sought to cauterize. I was bred a Catholic and a worldling, but the horrible persecution that I witnessed and the plot to introduce a worse than Spanish Inquisition which I learned from the King of France, made me resolve in my soul to rest not till I had chased from the land these locusts of Spain."

He proudly admitted the charge of being a demagogue, a flatterer of the people. "I confess that I am, and whilst life remains, shall ever be on the popular side, in the sense that I shall maintain the people's freedom and privileges." He scorned the king's setting a price on his head. "Does he think he will frighten me by this, when I know how for years I have been surrounded by his hired assassins and poisoners? Does he think he can ennoble my assassin? If this be the road to nobility in Castile, there is not a gentleman in the world, among nations that know what is true nobility, who would hold converse with so cowardly a miscreant." The document concluded with an impassioned peroration to the Dutch States-General, whom he addressed throughout the *Apology*, and with the promise: "Whatsoever you resolve for the good and the preservation of yourselves, your wives and children, and all that you hold sacred, I shall maintain, 'Je maintiendrai.'"

The reply of the northern States to the ban was their formal abjuration of the sovereign. In an Act of July 26, 1581, they solemnly renounced their allegiance to the King of Spain. A prince of the land, they declared, is appointed by God to rule his subjects even as a shepherd keeps his sheep; the subjects are not created by God for the benefit of the prince. If, then, the shepherd proves a tyrant, the subjects have a natural right to depose him, the more so when no other means is left to them to preserve their native freedom, in whose defense they are in duty bound, according to the law of nature, to sacrifice both life and property.

The historian Strada, of the Society of Jesus, who was horrified by this bold defiance of monarchy, wrote that the heavens signified their wrath by a terrific earthquake. The Act of Abjuration was, indeed, the first spasm of a tremor that was to revolutionize the body politic of Europe. When Charles I, in 1649, and Louis XVI, in the following century, were beheaded on the scaffold, it was the doctrine first formulated and put into practice by the Dutch that sealed their doom. When the American colonies proclaimed their independence, they did so in terms that voiced ideas enunciated, two hundred years earlier, by Prince William of Orange. "Though all should fail us," he wrote in 1574, "we shall at least have earned the honor of having done what no other nation did before us." In that honor is the secret of his triumph. It compelled the world's recognition of his ideas of political and religious liberty, which he championed on behalf of the Dutch people at the sacrifice of his noble life.

CHAPTER V

The Dutch Republic

IN WRITING the history of the Netherlands one is forced by the nature of the events to draw a gradually narrowing outline around the territory surveyed. At the beginning the Low Countries had no individual existence; they only counted as a part, and an inconspicuous one, of the Roman Empire. After its dissolution, their destinies were interwoven with those of the realm of the Franks. When that was broken up, their lot was cast within the framework of partly French and partly German history. Then, with the rise to power of the Burgundian dukes, the Low Countries were pried loose from Germany and France and their fortunes bound up with those of the Burgundian realm. With the Dutch revolt against Philip II they emerged, at last, as a distinct political entity. But the process of contraction did not end even there. The Union of Utrecht drew a dividing line between north and south, on either side of which the two were compelled by subsequent events to maintain and develop their separate lives. From then on, Dutch history is concerned with that territory only that now constitutes the kingdom of the Netherlands. What happened, after that break, in the southern provinces is Belgian history.

Biography shows a similar shrinkage. The author starts from the family's origin and rise in the world, discusses the fortunes of his hero's ancestry, then narrows down the story to his parental home, and finally, when he reaches manhood and enters upon the career that brought him fame, the narrative restricts itself to him alone. If the hero is one of a pair of twins, the biographer may treat their lives as a unit for a short period after they break away from home, but even the twin brother will drop out of the picture as each begins to make a name for himself in the world.

Holland and Belgium are twins who came to the parting of the ways in the eighties of the sixteenth century. The Dutch then living probably did not realize that it was a parting. In their eyes the Pacification of Ghent was a pact of greater historical significance than the Union of Utrecht. But the latter endured for more than two centuries; the former proved an ephemeral document of state.

Philip II had expected that all resistance in the Netherlands would collapse with Prince William's removal from the scene of action. But the insurgents in the north showed no sign of discouragement or despair. Providence provided them with a leader of the caliber of the murdered prince in Johan van Oldenbarnevelt, Lord Advocate of the province of Holland. This functionary was the legal adviser and spokesman of the delegation from the nobility to the assembly of the States of Holland. In that capacity he was the first to cast his vote, he asked the other deputies for their opinion, which was easily influenced by his own, he drew up the agenda for each meeting, he opened, read, and answered the letters of the envoys abroad. These functions gave him a powerful position in the assembly of the States-General and made him the leader of their foreign policy.

In his conduct of that policy he followed the line marked out by the Prince of Orange. The latter had planned to offer King Henry III of France the sovereignty that the King of Spain had forfeited. Henry III, however, declined the offer, whereupon Oldenbarnevelt, as leader of an embassy, sailed in 1585 to London to make the same presentation to Queen Elizabeth.

The queen also refused. But the very peril in which the

Union found itself at that juncture proved an asset to Oldenbarnevelt's policy. For the Spanish were scoring successes on land that threatened the newly won freedom of the Seven United Netherlands. Alexander Farnese, Prince of Parma, had been appointed governor of the Low Countries in 1578. He was an able diplomat and strategist, and what the great Duke of Alva had not been able to achieve with violence and terror, he accomplished with moderation and skillful strategy. Riots by Calvinist radicals in Flanders aided his campaign, for all Catholics in the south, and even the Reformed who dreaded mob rule, felt their ardor for the cause of the insurgents cool at the prospect of being dictated to by demagogues and extremists. Hence Parma met with only halfhearted resistance in the southern provinces. Ypres, Bruges, Ghent, Brussels, Mechelen surrendered one after another to his forces, and in 1585 the city of Antwerp, chief stronghold of the south, capitulated after a year's siege. With the great Scheldt port in his hands, Parma controlled the southern Netherlands. From that time on, the seven provinces in the north stood alone in their war against Spain.

But their peril was England's peril too. The queen was well aware that her island's safety was jeopardized if Spain recovered her rebel provinces and reinforced her strategic position on the opposite coast. She was not willing to go the length of challenging King Philip by the acceptance of the sovereignty that he considered his by the grace of God, but she did consent to aid the Dutch with six thousand men, in return for the surrender of Brielle, at the mouth of the Maas, and of Flushing and Fort Rammekens, at the mouth of the Scheldt, as security for the repayment of the cost of the expedition. The commander of the English troops, together with two other Englishmen, were to have seats in the Council of State and a say in the internal affairs of the confederacy. It was a high price to pay for England's military aid! In order to win their freedom from Spain, the United Provinces were willing to surrender part of that freedom to another power. Oldenbarnevelt himself had his misgivings as to the consequences of the treaty he had engineered. But Parma's military successes left him no alternative.

In December, 1585, Robert Dudley, Earl of Leicester, arrived in Holland as commander in chief of the English forces. The States-General, seeing in him the savior in their need, appointed him regent in opposition to Parma, who was the King of Spain's appointee. But whose sovereignty did the Earl of Leicester represent? Not the queen's, for she had declined to accept it. Nor that of the States-General, who were but an assembly of envoys from the individual provinces. Dutch jurisprudents, among them Hugo Grotius, were inclined to claim the sovereignty for the provincial States, but others argued in favor of the people as the true sovereign.

The Earl of Leicester, invested with the regency on behalf of an undefinable sovereign, made ill-advised use of his great power. Unfamiliar with Dutch conditions and unable to understand the people's mentality, he made one tactical mistake after another. First, he offended the States of Holland by choosing the city of Utrecht, because of its central location, for his residence. The province of Holland, which had borne the brunt of the war with Spain, and had made financial sacrifices far greater than those of the other members of the Union, felt itself slighted by the governor's refusal to reside within its territory. His next move struck a blow at Holland's sea-borne commerce. For he forbade all trading with the enemy, a prohibition that met with bitter opposition from the seaports of Holland, as it paralyzed their lucrative freight-carrying business. The shipowners argued that if they did not ship grain to Spanish harbors, others—the English, of course —would do it; Spain would not suffer a loss of supplies, but Holland would lose to Leicester's countrymen the freightage profits that helped to finance the war.

Oldenbarnevelt, who was appointed Lord Advocate in

1586, took the lead in opposing the regent. If Leicester had proved his mettle as commander in chief of his English forces, he might have weathered the political storm. But his troops were ill equipped, irregularly paid, and consequently undisciplined. Parma's military successes continued unabated. He entrenched himself on the Maas by the capture of Grave and Venlo, and frustrated the Earl of Leicester's attempt to wrest Zutphen and Sluis from the Spanish. Discredited as a military leader, and politically at odds with the most powerful of the United Provinces, he tried to regain his prestige by force. Oldenbarnevelt was to be imprisoned, the governments of Amsterdam and Leyden overthrown by his henchmen. But none of these attempts succeeded, and in December, 1587, two years after his triumphant arrival, he returned to England, disillusioned and disgraced.

His loss was Holland's gain. The conflict with the Earl of Leicester had been a test of its power and the States of the province had proved that they could not be defied with impunity. Oldenbarnevelt, the leader of their opposition, was, as a result of the regent's defeat, the most influential man in the Republic. The Hague, not Utrecht, had henceforth the undisputed distinction of being the seat of the federal government. Here the States-General were in continuous session; here also met the States of Holland; here resided the stadtholder of that province, who was stadtholder also of Zeeland, Utrecht, Gelderland, and Overijsel; here the Council of State held its deliberations. The Hague was henceforth the political capital of the Republic.

How that Republic had come into existence was a question that no one could answer with any degree of assurance. The Union of Utrecht had not created it, for at the time of its conclusion the provinces still recognized King Philip as their overlord. Nor did their abjuration of him, two years later, usher in the Republic. Their offer of the sovereignty to the King of France and the Queen of England is convincing proof that the Prince of Orange and Oldenbarnevelt did not look upon the Union as an independent commonwealth. The Dutch Republic was never planned, nor ever solemnly proclaimed. It came about through the compelling course of events, not willed, but imperceptibly evolved.

That haphazard genesis accounts for the many imperfections in its structure. It never became a unified state but remained a loose alliance of seven independent republics. The supreme authority within each province was lodged in the provincial States, an assembly of deputies from the nobility and the towns. Each province had its stadtholder, who, under Burgundian rule, had been the lieutenant governor for the absent sovereign. After the abjuration of the sovereign, in 1581, it would have been logical to abolish the office. However, the stadtholder was maintained as an appointee of the provincial States, upon which, according to Grotius' theory, the sovereignty had devolved. His chief function was the appointment of city magistrates from a double nomination submitted by the municipal councils. He was the nominal chief of the provincial courts of justice, and had the power to pardon criminals condemned to death. He was commander of the armed forces and the naval contingent of his province. In short, he performed practically the same functions that had been the stadtholder's in the Burgundian period. Prince William's son, Maurice, was appointed, after his father's death, to the office of stadtholder in five of the seven provinces, his cousin William Louis, Count of Nassau, in Friesland and Groningen. Maurice was also admiral general of the Union and commander in chief of the federal forces. And both stadtholders were members of the Council of State, the only leftover of the Burgundian administration in which its centralizing tendencies lingered on. For that very reason the provincial States, always jealous of their independence, were bent on curtailing its authority. They left the Council in charge of the maintenance of the fortresses along the frontiers of the Union, they let it prepare the annual war budget, and administer the federal finances with the assistance of a federal Chamber of Accounts. But they took away from the Council its principal function, the management of the Union's foreign affairs, and transferred it to the assembly of the States-General, which was a joint session of delegations from the seven assemblies of the provincial States. Each province guarded its sovereignty so jealously that no delegation was allowed to vote on any matter, however urgent, until it had traveled back to the provincial capital for all instructions. In the Council of State, Gelderland, Holland, Zeeland and Friesland were each represented by three, Utrecht, Overijsel, and Groningen by two councilors. None of these was under compulsion to vote according to orders, and all matters were decided by a majority of the members present. The other members of the Council were the two stadtholders and the three Englishmen. Prince Maurice, as the stadtholder of five provinces, and commander in chief of the federal army and navy, symbolized in his person the unity of the seven allies, which none of them was anxious to see either stressed or strengthened, and his membership of the Council was additional reason for the provinces to transfer its chief powers to the States-General. That so clumsy a machinery could function nevertheless was mainly due to the preponderance of Holland in the States-General, and to the skill and ability of Oldenbarnevelt and some of his successors, whose forceful leadership supplied the lack of co-ordination.

The events that brought the Republic into existence were not wholly of a political nature. Military successes had a share in that evolutionary process. From 1590 on the war against Spain took a turn for the better, thanks to a thorough reorganization of the army of the confederacy. That army was not recruited from the people. The towns had their civic guards for self-protection, but Prince William's campaigns had been fought with bands of mercenaries, soldiers of fortune from various countries, but chiefly of German nationality. They were an ill-disciplined lot. When they did not receive their pay on time—which happened all too often—they were less dangerous to the enemy than to the people they were supposed to defend.

Prince Maurice, the commander in chief, drilled these unruly bands into a modern army. With the financial backing of the province of Holland he made regular payment a fixed rule, and saw to it that his troops were well supplied with food and equipment and properly housed in decent barracks. But in return he demanded and enforced an iron discipline. In this way he built up a strong army whose striking force was demonstrated in the campaigns of 1590 and following years, which cleared the territory of the United Provinces of Spanish troops before the close of the century.

That same decade was a period of unexampled activity at sea. It would seem as if the Hollanders were spurred on by their hard-won deliverance from tyranny to venture on ever more daring exploits. The favorable wind of success blew upon their sails and sent them into regions where Dutch commerce had never done business before, to the Mediterranean, to Russia, and the fabulous Indies. Until the eighties they had obtained the spices of the Moluccas from Portugal. But King Philip, for whom the Duke of Alva had conquered Portugal in 1580, began to close the Portuguese harbors to Dutch traders and confiscate ships that dared disregard the ban. The time came when he was to regret this ill-advised policy. For he soon discovered that he could not save his people from starving without the grain imported by Dutch freighters. Though the embargo remained on the statute books, the grain ships from Holland resumed their deliveries with the connivance of the Spanish customs. And meanwhile the Hollanders, prevented from buying the Moluccan spices in Portugal, sailed for the Indies to get them at first hand. In 1595 three ships under Cornelis de Houtman reached Java, and when they returned to Amsterdam, two years later, the church bells were tolled throughout the city to welcome them home. It was, indeed, an auspicious event, for it inaugurated Holland's colonial enterprise.

The success of De Houtman's expedition spurred others on to risk ships and crews in voyages to the Far East. Shipowners entered into partnerships to finance a Moluccan venture. So many rival companies were competing for the Indian trade at the beginning of the new century that Oldenbarnevelt, foreseeing that lack of cohesion would make them powerless to resist the Spaniards, persuaded the competitors, all stubborn upholders of free trade, to stave off their common ruin by renouncing for once their faith in its blessings, and pool their several interests in an East India Company. In March, 1602, the States-General granted the merger a charter for twenty-one years, which gave it a monopoly of trade with all countries east of the Cape of Good Hope and west of the Strait of Magellan, with powers of sovereignty throughout that region of the globe, including the right to wage war and conclude peace.

Plans for a West India Company which was to be its counterpart in the Western Hemisphere were proposed a decade later by Willem Usselincx, a refugee merchant from Antwerp. But Oldenbarnevelt would not consent to these. Private monopolies were injurious, he explained, to the welfare of the country and its inhabitants. He had swerved from that standpoint, it is true, when he promoted the formation of the East India Company, but that was done under the stress of war, in order that the interests engaged in the Moluccan trade might oppose a united front to the Spanish in the Far East. But in 1609 the States-General had concluded a twelve years' truce with the enemy, and everything, therefore, should be avoided that might egg the Spanish on to a resumption of hostilities.

That truce was the work of Oldenbarnevelt and the merchant rulers of Holland. These were eager for peace and an undisturbed flow of sea-borne trade. But the truce was not popular with the zealous among the Reformed, least of all with the thousands of Calvinist refugees from the southern Netherlands, who wanted the war continued until their provinces too had been freed from Spanish tyranny. They decried the truce as an act of treason, a cynical deal of Holland's moneyed interests at the expense of the enslaved south. The Calvinist ministers would have no dealings with the enemy either, for they feared that any relaxation of the war against Spain would lead to a revival of Catholicism. Nor did Prince Maurice approve of the truce. As commander of the federal army he considered his military mission only partly fulfilled as long as the south remained under Spanish rule, and the truce interrupted the work of liberation.

Still, the truce with Spain was a signal victory for the Seven United Provinces. For King Philip III, without formally recognizing their independence, negotiated with them "as if they were a free and sovereign state." And only eleven years previously his father, Philip II, had presented all the Netherlands, both north and south, as a wedding gift to his daughter Isabel on the occasion of her marriage to Albert, Archduke of Austria, whom the king had appointed his regent. That had been, from Philip II's point of view, a clever move. He promised the Low Countries autonomy as a bait for their submission to the regent's rule. That would obviate, he thought, their aversion to being under foreign domination, yet they would not be lost to Spain if the marriage of Albert and Isabel remained childless, as in that case the Low Countries would revert to the Spanish crown. The southern provinces, already resigned to their resubmission to Spanish authority, were easily reconciled to this new arrangement that gave them a semblance of self-rule under the archduke. But the northern Netherlands could not be coaxed by that promising word into surrender of their new-won freedom. They continued the war, both on land and sea, until Spain herself, financially exhausted, sued for a truce, which she was willing to buy even at the price of virtual recognition of their independence. From 1609 on, the confederacy in the north was in fact, if not in name, a free and self-sufficient state, which in the ensuing decades was to evolve into a continental power of the first magnitude.

But cessation of hostilities did not bring peace to the Netherlands. As soon as the shooting ceased, internal strife began. Religious dissension brought the country to the verge of civil war. The orthodox and the modernists within the Reformed Church clashed over the doctrine of predestination. The trouble started with a dispute between two Leyden professors, Arminius, who rejected predestination, and Gomarus, upholder of Calvinist orthodoxy. The Arminians appealed for support to the States of Holland. These forbade the ministers to discuss the controversial doctrine in the pulpit, to the great indignation of the Gomarists, who denied to the secular authority the right to dictate to the church. Oldenbarnevelt and the majority in the States of Holland wanted the matter submitted to a provincial synod, but the Gomarists, well aware that the Arminians had no following outside Holland, insisted upon the calling of a federal synod in which all the provinces would be represented. In this way the theological controversy became a nation-wide conflict of political import, as it involved the vexing question whether the authority of the individual provinces or that of the States-General was paramount.

Prince Maurice, as the commander of the federal army and as stadtholder of five of the seven provinces, was naturally a champion of federal as against provincial supremacy. He was not concerned with the religious implications of the quarrel. He was a soldier, not a theologian. Bitterness over his military inactivity, to which he was doomed by the truce, may also have played its part in inducing him to head the Gomarist faction, since Oldenbarnevelt favored the Arminian cause. Envious rivals and disappointed suitors of the Advocate found satisfaction for their grudges in rallying to the support of Maurice, thus injecting the acidity of personal hatred into a conflict that was envenomed by religious intolerance from the start.

In August, 1617, the States of Holland, under the leadership of Oldenbarnevelt, adopted a resolution that empowered the cities of that province to levy their own troops of mercenaries, *waardgelders,* so called, and ordered the officers and soldiers of the federal army to obey, on pain of dismissal, not Prince Maurice, their commander in chief, but the authorities of the towns in which they were garrisoned. This action was a reduction to absurdity of the doctrine of states' rights as against the supreme power of the confederacy. For Oldenbarnevelt and his supporters, including the great jurist, Hugo Grotius, then Pensionary of Rotterdam, claimed for their province the right of rebellion against the Union which each of the seven had sworn to uphold against Spain. It was a tactical mistake on their parts which gave Maurice a faint semblance of justification for his contention that resistance to Oldenbarnevelt was tantamount to resisting Spain. "Spanje of Oranje," Spain or Orange, was the rhyming slogan under which he rallied the orthodox Calvinists around his banner. The rhyme made the false antithesis popular, and daily repetition made it seem true.

In the summer of 1618 the States-General, over the protests of the delegations from Holland and Utrecht, voted by a majority of five to two to summon a federal synod. Maurice was given power to discharge the *waardgelders* in the city of Utrecht and to replace Oldenbarnevelt's supporters in the municipal government by stanch upholders of orthodox Calvinism. He met with only vocal opposition. The mercenaries obeyed almost sheepishly his order to disband, the city council was combed clean of rebel elements, and the States of the province gave their consent to a federal synod.

Holland was isolated, after the loss of Utrecht's support; and even within his own province Oldenbarnevelt had to cope with a Calvinist minority opposed to the foolhardy course he was steering. Even among his faithful followers there were signs of defection. They saw the handwriting on the wall and were for yielding to Maurice before it was too late. Pleased with the prince's skillful discharge of his mission to Utrecht, the States-General decided to give him dictatorial powers. In a secret session, to which no delegates from Holland were admitted, he was authorized to take such measures as he deemed called for by the emergency. He acted immediately. The next day Oldenbarnevelt, Hugo Grotius, and the two leaders of their faction at Leyden and Utrecht were placed under arrest and in fourteen towns of Holland the Arminians were removed from the government.

The four leaders were tried before a federal court especially constituted for the occasion. It was made up of twenty-four judges, twelve from Holland, two from each of the six other provinces. Some of them were personal enemies of Oldenbarnevelt. They found the accused guilty of high treason in conspiring to disturb the peace and unity of the Republic and condemned the Lord Advocate to death. As if they were anxious to justify the passage of so severe a sentence, they enumerated in the lengthy verdict all actions that could be construed, by fair means or foul, as treasonable or dangerous to the safety of the state; they even implied that in negotiating the twelve-year truce he had intended to betray the country to Spain. Grotius and Hogerbeets, the pensionary of Leyden, were condemned to imprisonment for life. The third, the pensionary of Utrecht, had committed suicide in prison, but even in death he did not escape the judges' revengeful severity. His estate was confiscated, along with those of his fellow convicts.

The Lord Advocate's death sentence was executed the following day. "Do not believe that I am a traitor to my country," he said to the people surrounding the scaffold. The next moment he knelt and offered his neck to the executioner's sword.

Meanwhile the federal synod had convened at Dordrecht and had condemned the Arminian interpretation of Calvin's doctrine. In accordance with that verdict, the States-General forbade the Arminian ministers the pulpit, and those who refused to obey were banished from the country. They also gave effect to another vote of the synod which, in the light of our afterknowledge, appears of far greater significance. The synod adopted a resolution calling for the translation of the Bible from the Hebrew and the Greek, which was to be the official text of the Dutch Reformed Church, and the States-General set the work on this project in motion by promptly voting the necessary appropriation. The new version, the joint labor of twelve translators and twelve correctors, was completed by 1634. The States Bible, as it was called, became the treasured household book of every Dutch home. It has been a source of comfort and devotion to successive generations, a model of style to Dutch writers, and a unifying force between the speakers of the various provincial dialects in that it taught them one common language in which to pray and worship God.

The triumph of the Calvinists under the leadership of Maurice was, indeed, a step forward in the direction of unity. The Lord Advocate's tragic death on the scaffold, after forty years of untiring and devoted service to the state, was a terrible sacrifice to pay for even so desirable an end. Unity had also been his goal. But he envisaged unity achieved through the supremacy of Holland over the other six provinces. Holland, in his time, had always taken the lead. If it had not been for Holland, the resistance against Spain would have collapsed. Holland with her wealth, fruit of her industry and commerce, had borne the risks and the financial burdens of the war. There was, according to his way of thinking, no safety and no freedom for the other provinces except under the aegis of Holland. But the Prince of Orange strove for unity through joint action of seven equals that expressed their common will in the assembly of the States-General. Not six under one, but seven together. "I am sentenced in an age which has other maxims of state than the age in which I lived," was Oldenbarnevelt's comment on the verdict of his twenty-four judges. There was, indeed, no guilt of treason on his part. There was a clash of policies, and the party that had the backing of the majority and of the military power won, with the victory, the right of punishment. The Lord Advocate's chief fault was his overweening confidence, which blinded him to the risks he was taking and to the certainty of his defeat.

The power of the stadtholder was greatly enhanced by the outcome of the conflict. As commander of the federal army and stadtholder of five of the seven provinces, he was the embodiment of that conception of federal unity that he had brought to triumph over the one that Oldenbarnevelt had stood for. The office of Lord Advocate of Holland was shorn of part of its prerogatives. Oldenbarnevelt's successor was no longer entrusted with the foreign correspondence of the States-General, and his term of office was limited to a period of five years. And as if the victorious party were anxious to efface all connection of the new functionary's office with the memory of his great predecessor, the title of Pensionary was substituted for that of Lord Advocate.

The twelve-year truce expired in 1621. But Spain, by that time, had become involved in the civil war that had been waging since 1618 between Catholics and Protestants in Germany, and lacked the will and the means to resume the fighting in the Netherlands with the needed vigor. And Maurice, who had no longer the energy and the health of thirty years earlier—he died in 1625—remained on the defensive. Greater activity was shown in overseas regions. The death of Oldenbarnevelt and the approaching end of the truce had given Usselincx a chance to press his plans for a West India Company. It was founded in 1621 and received a monopoly of trade with all countries west of the Cape of Good Hope and east of the Strait of Magellan, with untrammeled license to wage war on the enemy in his American colonies and prey on his ships in American waters.

The planting of colonies was another item on Usselincx's program. He was an ardent Calvinist, and war against Spain was to him identical with war against Rome. He hoped to strike a blow at the former's commercial interests in America and at the latter by spreading the Reformed religion through Protestant settlers. The founding of New Amsterdam on Manhattan in 1624 was, therefore, an act of war against both.

Dutch interest in Manhattan and the great river that flowed seaward past its western shore had been aroused by Henry Hudson's famous voyage in the *Half Moon*. His ship was owned by a group of Amsterdam merchants, and the expedition he headed was one in a series of attempts to find a northeast passage through the arctic seas to China and the East Indies, beyond the reach of the enemy's patrolling men-of-war. Previous attempts had ended in failure. The most famous of these was Willem Barents' third and last voyage. Its chief result was the discovery of the island that he christened Spitsbergen. He did not live to bring the news to Amsterdam. For after wintering on Novaya Zemlya he left his icebound ship to her fate and set out with his crew in two open boats. Most of the party reached home, but Barents himself died and was given a grave in the arctic seas.

Hudson's search for the northeast passage was equally futile. Disobeying his employers' instructions to return if he failed in piloting the *Half Moon* through the ice, he sailed straight west in hope of reaching the Far East around the north of America. And thus he discovered the river that has since borne his name.

By September 1, 1623 a capital of more than seven million guilders had been invested in the West India Company, and in June, 1626, Peter Minuit made his famous purchase of Manhattan Island. By that time the town of New Amsterdam had been laid out, the fort was building, the colonists were settled. But through that purchase the accomplished fact of occupation acquired a semblance of justice which the Amsterdam directors were anxious to lend to their enterprise. For it was in obedience to their orders that Minuit paid the value of sixty florins to the Indians.

The settlement in North America was only a minor concern of the company. The Republic was at war with Spain and the company's first duty was to carry that war into the Spanish colonies. Its chief efforts, therefore, were directed against the West Indies and South America. In the thirties the company ousted the Spanish from Olinda and the Recife in Brazil, conquered St. Eustatius and Curaçao, and wrested St. George del Mina, on the coast of West Africa, from the enemy. John Maurice, Count of Nassau, a grandson of William of Orange's brother John, was appointed Governor of Brazil in 1637, and during his seven years of office the Dutch extended their hold on the coast of Brazil from the Rio Grande in the south to the Island of Maranhão in the north. His conquests meant for the Portuguese colonists merely an exchange of unwelcome masters. They hated the Dutch heretics, but they hated their Spanish oppressors no less. But the many Jewish settlers were better off under John Maurice's tolerant rule than under the Spaniards.

The company's chief profits, however, came not from commerce with its settlements but from piracy. Its fleets preyed on the galleons that carried gold and silver from the mines in South America to Spanish ports. In 1628 a Dutch fleet of thirty-one ships under Piet Heyn intercepted the treasure fleet off the coast of Cuba, and forced the crews to surrender their precious cargo, representing a value of over eleven million guilders. But such quickly won wealth had a demoralizing effect on the directors at home. The slower process of colonization, which might yield profits, perhaps, to their sons or grandsons, had less attraction for them. Greed that lusted for immediate returns proved the bane of the company's colonial enterprise.

In 1640 the Portuguese, after sixty years of submission to Spain, rose in revolt, and proclaimed John of Braganza king. This action made Portugal a virtual ally of the Republic, and in the following year they actually concluded a pact under which the States-General promised aid to Portugal in return for the latter's consent to the maintenance of the status quo outside Europe. But the Portuguese in Brazil were not willing to have their own freedom bartered for the security of the mother land. Hostilities broke out, in which the weakness of the company's hold on the colony was revealed. John Maurice, having insisted in vain on stronger support from the directors, resigned his office in disgust and returned to Holland in 1644. Within a few years the entire colony was lost to the Dutch.

The East India Company, on the other hand, was making better use of its sovereign rights. Its governor general, Jan Pieterszoon Coen (1618–23 and again 1627–29), had moved the company's headquarters from the Moluccas to West Java, where in 1619 he had captured and destroyed the native stronghold of Jacatra and built Batavia on its ruins. He was the founder of Holland's colonial power in the Far East. A ruthless, energetic ruler and zealous servant, according to the Calvinist creed, of the Lord Almighty, he never doubted but the hand of God was guiding him in all he did to establish the rule of his company and of his God among the heathen. Together with the English, he ousted the Portuguese from their island footholds, persuaded native princes to grant the company the exclusive right of trading with their territories, and created in their minds an awesome conception of the power and the greatness of the white nation that sent him.

In 1623 he resigned his office and sailed for home. But four years later he was prevailed upon by the directors to return. The Dutch and English, once allied against the Portuguese, were now at loggerheads. The Hollanders on the island of Amboina in the Moluccas had put a number of Englishmen to death on a charge of conspiracy. The English raised the cry of "murder!" Collaboration between them and the Dutch was no longer possible. From allies they became enemies, and all Coen's determination was needed to safeguard the company's interests and his own creation. That Amboina verdict left a bitter taste in English mouths. Half a century later it was not yet forgotten. Dryden was to dramatize it and arouse, with his play, the Briton's will to war against the wicked Dutch.

The incident was, indeed, galling for British pride. That upstart nation, which had begged their queen for help forty years earlier, had the impudence to sentence and execute His Majesty's subjects! It was that impudence, rather than the cruelty, that riled them. For it was a symptom of a new self-assurance in these Hollanders, of which they had not been capable in Queen Elizabeth's days.

They showed it on other occasions. In 1626 the States-General decided to bar the British ambassador from the Council of State. His right to membership in that body was part of the security that Queen Elizabeth had exacted for her military aid. But Oldenbarnevelt, availing himself of King James's urgent need of money, had offered him £250,000 for the Republic's release from all its indebtedness, and the king, though he had demanded three times that amount, had accepted. As a result, the English garrisons had been withdrawn from Brielle,

Flushing, and Rammekens, and the States-General were fully within their rights when they demanded the withdrawal also of the ambassador from the Council of State.

During the reign of King Charles I, British naval pride was stung to the quick by Dutch disregard of England's sovereignty within her home waters. In 1639, a Spanish armada, badly mauled by the Dutch under Marten Harpertszoon Tromp, sought refuge in the Downs. Tromp sent the Spanish admiral challenge after challenge to come out and fight; but not receiving any response, he went to the attack and all but destroyed the enemy's fleet within sight of an English squadron.

The States-General showed themselves equally self-reliant in their dealings with France. They concluded, in 1624, a treaty with France which the Calvinist ministers decried as an unholy pact with the devil. Richelieu's government had laid siege to La Rochelle, the chief stronghold of the Huguenots, and the States undertook, in return for a subsidy, to aid the French army by attacking the city from the sea. The States-General were in a painful dilemma: if they recalled their fleet, they would incur Richelieu's anger; if they did not, they faced Calvinist discontent at home. They evidently feared the ministers' enmity more than the cardinal's, for they called their naval squadron home.

Richelieu's political aim was to weaken the power of the House of Hapsburg by opposing the emperor in his war against the Protestants in Germany. The cardinal, therefore, saw in the Protestant powers on the Continent his natural allies against the hereditary enemy of France. He could afford to overlook the Republic's defection in the case of La Rochelle if by his forbearance he gained the support of the United Provinces in a greater cause. He persuaded Gustavus Adolphus, King of Sweden, to invade Germany, and guaranteed to the States-General an annual subsidy of half a million guilders so they might press the war against Spain.

Prince Frederick Henry, meanwhile, had succeeded his step-brother Maurice as stadtholder and commander in chief of the federal army. He had scored a signal success, in 1628, by the capture of Bois-le-Duc, which gave him control of the whole of North Brabant, and, after the pact with France of 1630, he conquered in a dashing campaign other strongholds higher up along the Maas—Venlo, Roermond, and Maastricht—thus adding the province of Limburg to his conquests.

After the death of Gustavus Adolphus, who fell in the battle of Lützen in 1632, the Hapsburg forces in Germany rallied from the blows they had suffered. The imperial army under the emperor's son Ferdinand dealt a crushing blow to the Swedes at Nördlingen in 1634. A defeat of the Protestant cause in the empire would jeopardize the freedom of the Republic. The States-General sent envoys to Paris to negotiate closer military co-operation with France. Their mission was successful. In 1635 the United Provinces concluded with France an alliance for mutual support. France would declare war on Spain, each power would maintain a field force of twenty-five thousand foot and five thousand horse, and neither could make peace without the other.

The aim of the allies was the reconquest of the southern Netherlands. These had reverted to the Spanish crown by the death of Archduchess Isabel in 1638. They were to be wrested from Spain and divided between the two victors. But nothing came of this ambitious plan. The war dragged on with alternating successes and setbacks. War weariness on either side made for a stalemate. In Holland especially the clamor for peace gained in urgency from year to year. Various motives prompted the merchant rulers of that province to insist on a cessation of hostilities. They hoped, first of all, for a business boom with the return to normalcy. Peace, in the second place, would reduce the power and prestige of the Prince of Orange, who seemed to forget that he was not a sovereign monarch but merely a servant and appointee of the provincial States. And lastly, they were not too anxious to win France for a neighbor.

They would rather keep her at a safe distance, with the southern Netherlands under Spain as a buffer state between them. In consequence, the prince's war effort did not receive wholehearted backing from the most powerful province of the Union.

In 1646 delegates of the Republic, Spain, and France assembled in Münster and began peace negotiations that dragged on for two years. The Spanish envoys offered the Dutch the most generous terms, but refused to yield to the French demands. The Republic's delegates, under pressure from Holland, fell for the bait and concluded with Spain a separate peace, such as the United Provinces were bound by their treaty with France not to conclude. They had tried, it is true, to effect a reconciliation between the two kingdoms. When all their efforts failed, however, they found it impossible not to accept the Spanish terms. These gave them complete independence from Spain, and King Philip IV pledged his word that he would obtain recognition of that independence from the emperor. Each party would retain the territories held at the cessation of hostilities, both in Europe and overseas, and Spain agreed not to extend her possessions in the Indies.

Thus liberty was attained eighty years after William of Orange took up arms in defense of the Dutch people. More was achieved than he had envisaged. For the United Provinces had not only shaken off the Spanish yoke, but had also severed the ties that bound them to the German Empire. The Burgundian Kreis had only led a nominal existence, but even that name had now been canceled. The Dutch Republic was recognized by king and emperor, and by the world at large, as a free and sovereign state and as one of the great powers of the Continent.

CHAPTER VI

Dutch-English Rivalry

THE PEACE negotiations at Münster were part of a larger conference in which envoys from nearly all the sovereigns of the Continent participated. Only Russia, Poland, and Denmark were not represented. So large was the concourse of delegates, and so difficult the problem of precedence among them, that this European congress was split into two sections, one meeting in Münster, the other in Osnabrück. The body of settlements arrived at, including the treaty between the Dutch Republic and Spain, is known as the Peace of Westphalia. All Protestant and Roman Catholic countries that had been involved in the Thirty and Eighty Years' wars came to terms with one another in a futile attempt to inaugurate an era of peace.

France and Spain alone could not agree. The war between them dragged on for nearly another decade. But in 1659 Mazarin succeeded in negotiating the peace treaty of the Pyrenees, which made it clear to everybody that France had become the first power in the world. Spain emerged from the war so utterly exhausted that in the following years she sought the friendship of the Dutch Republic as the one state in Europe that could help her resist French aggression in the southern Netherlands.

The menace of an all-powerful France sharing a common frontier with the United Provinces had been averted by the latter's separate peace with Spain. They had averted it, indeed, by breaking their pledge to France and exposing themselves to Mazarin's vengeance. But they preferred having their beaten enemy for a neighbor to living next door to an ambitious friend, and risked the latter's enmity rather than help him annex the southern Netherlands which, in the hands of Spain, formed a convenient buffer state.

The Peace of Westphalia was as unpopular with the Calvinists as the twelve-year truce had been, especially with those whose original home was in the south. As a sop to them the Catholics, under the treaty, were refused public worship in the Netherlands, a departure from the tolerant policy Prince William had always advocated. The merchant rulers of Holland, though equally liberal minded, gave in on this point for political reasons. They did not mean to, and never did, enforce the ban with uncompromising severity.

The stanch supporters of the Prince of Orange were not too well pleased with the peace treaty either. Frederick Henry died a year before the final pact was signed; but his young son, Prince William II, ambitious and impetuous, made a bold attempt to reverse the peace policy of Holland's merchant class and resume the war with Spain on the side of France. He even risked internal strife by using federal troops against the city of Amsterdam; only by yielding to the threat of force did the burgomasters avert civil war. His outspoken opponents in the governments of the cities of Holland were forced out of office, a few of their leaders imprisoned, and the prince, now feeling himself the unchallenged arbiter of the Republic's policies, pursued an ever more reckless course. If he could have his way, it was feared in Holland, he would invade the southern Netherlands, go to the aid of the Stuarts to avenge the murder of his father-in-law, King Charles I, and, aggrandized by his military triumphs, establish a monarchy in the Netherlands. But his ambitious dreams, if such they were, came to naught. He died in 1650 of smallpox, in his twenty-fourth year, survived by his English widow and a posthumously born son.

His sudden death gave the rulers of Holland the chance they

had been waiting for. Since Oldenbarnevelt's political defeat, the Prince of Orange, supported by the States-General, had wielded supreme power in the Republic. There was no one who could exercise authority such as his, except the States of the most powerful province. Holland invited the six other provinces to send their complete States assemblies to The Hague for a special meeting in which the confederates could discuss their common problems. A double purpose would be served by this expansion of the States-General far beyond normal size. Their permanent session, which met daily, was packed with partisans and creatures of the Prince of Orange; in the larger conference these would present a less formidable bloc. And the full presence of the seven assemblies would make it unnecessary for the provincial delegates to return home for guidance as to how they should vote.

But not one of the six provinces sent its States Assembly. Only large delegations appeared, so that the extraordinary meeting, the Great Assembly as it was called, proved merely a duplicate of the States-General, which was also in session at the same time. No weighty decisions were taken. The chief outcome of the long-drawn-out deliberations was a reorganization of the federal army in accordance with Holland's wishes. Disintegration would be a more appropriate term. For the individual provinces were given the right to interfere with the decisions of the army command. No troops might in future be moved into or out of any province without the consent of the States Assembly of that province, and all such troop movements, formerly decided upon by the commander in chief, were henceforth ordered by the States-General. Appointments of officers were to be made by the States of the province responsible for the upkeep of their troops, and all soldiers had to swear an oath of allegiance not only to the States-General but also to the States of that province that gave them their pay. And if the troops were not in the pay of the province into which they were moved, the States of this other province, and even the municipal rulers of their garrison towns, had also to be included in their oath.

Since Holland disbursed more for the maintenance of the army than the six other provinces together, the States of that province had the larger part of the Republic's armed forces at their disposal. If any unity of command was preserved, it came from Holland's financial preponderance. But in essence the Republic's forces were a coalition of seven little armies, each in the pay and under the orders of a diminutive sovereign commonwealth that was an ally of the six others. Oldenbarnevelt's conception of the Republic had triumphed a generation after his ignominious death. Holland's influence alone held the self-willed allies together. It would require great skill and wisdom to steer the seven ships of state as a unit through the stormy seas of European politics.

Fortunately there was a leader of men in Holland who possessed the wisdom and skill required for that task. Jan de Witt was Pensionary of Dordrecht at the time of the Great Assembly, and as head of that city's deputation he had a hand in the framing of its resolutions. In 1653 he was called to the higher office of Pensionary of Holland, at the very time when that province reasserted its claim to first rank among its equals and could exercise its power without fear of obstruction by the Prince of Orange.

De Witt was a typical representative of his class, son of a patrician family that for more than two centuries had played a role in the government of Holland's oldest city, Dordrecht. His grandfather had been a stanch supporter of Prince William, and after his death, of Oldenbarnevelt. He and his like thought of themselves as the true defenders of Dutch liberty. They had vindicated it with the Prince of Orange against King Philip, they had stood by Oldenbarnevelt to maintain it against another Prince of Orange, whose ambitious grasp for monarchic power, so they thought, had threatened to undo his own father's creation. For true liberty, as they saw it, was best safeguarded under a government composed of the best minds of the nation, and these were to be found among the merchant rulers of the cities of Holland, who through their international commerce had acquired a wide and varied knowledge of men and affairs and the determination that dares assert its will over others.

They were broad-minded men in an age that understood only intolerance and prejudice. The liberal humanism of Erasmus appealed to them, not the rigorous tenets of Calvin, to which they paid lip service as members of the Dutch Reformed Church. Hence the ministers of that church were often critical of the authorities, and sometimes used their influence upon the masses to arouse them to demonstrations against some policy that the church did not favor. It was part of their tolerant regime not to suppress such criticism of their rule. In 1581, an ordinance was issued in the name, but not by order, of the Prince of Orange prohibiting the printing and selling of all manner of scandalous, abusive, and seditious books and pamphlets without the permission of the magistracy. It was never put into execution in any town of Holland, and the Leyden magistrates even refused to have it proclaimed in their city. Instead, they issued a remonstrance addressed to the synod of Middelburg, from whose midst it was well known that this attempt at preventive censorship had emanated. "Liberty," they wrote, "has always consisted in uttering our sentiments freely; and the contrary has always been considered the characteristic of tyranny. Reason, which is the adversary of all tyrants, teaches us that truth can be as little restrained as light."

The ruling class in the Dutch Republic was not a caste of tyrants. The discussion of political issues, the criticism of government in town and province, even personal attacks on men in office, were ignored rather than restrained. The people, intent on their individual pursuits, were satisfied to let the upper ten run the country, but they insisted on their right to air their grievances. The men in power knew the national temper too well not to respect their insistence on that freedom. It happened occasionally that an all too bold pamphleteer was prosecuted and his seditious book confiscated; now and then the authorities issued a warning against excesses committed in print by certain libelous writers. But such cases were the exceptions. The annals of the Dutch Republic are not stained by any records of authors pilloried for their outspokenness or of printers punished with the loss of their ears for daring to publish seditious matter. In maintaining such freedom for the written word in the midst of a censor-ridden Europe, the rulers of the Republic were ahead of their age.

Unrepressed discussion of public affairs supplied a brake to the autocratic power of the oligarchy. Though the masses did not rule and had little to say, they could bring pressure to bear upon those who ruled them. The historian Hooft, himself a member of a ruling Amsterdam family and an aristocrat by temper and breeding, wrote in the thirties of the seventeenth century: "In this country the greatest changes were brought about through the instigation or, at any rate, through the active compulsion of the common man; and in these days not the least art of the municipal government consists in managing and placating the multitude."

De Witt, as Pensionary of Holland, was no longer concerned with municipal government. The province and the Union were his field of action, and the scope and meaning of affairs within that wider sphere eluded the understanding of the man in the street. Yet even there the multitude sometimes sought to assert its adverse opinion and will. The Prince of Orange, whether his name were William, Maurice, or Frederick Henry, had the unswerving loyalty of the Calvinist masses. These were resigned to a stadtholderless government during the minority of the young prince, but De

Witt's determination to exclude him permanently from all offices held by his ancestors bred widespread resentment, the expression of which in speech and print grew in vehemence as the prince approached his majority.

De Witt's opposition to the House of Orange was a matter of family tradition. His father had been among the chief opponents of Prince William II and had suffered imprisonment in Loevesteyn Castle for attempting to thwart his pro-French war policy. The son neither forgot nor forgave. The memory of his father's disgrace convinced him that there could be no freedom under a one-man rule. The hereditary rights of a dynasty were dangerous to Dutch liberty. He despised the emotional masses that worshiped the prince in blind ignorance of what was best for them. He described himself as "a wise and stern father who, if he should yield to the will and inclinations of his children, would be likely to do them serious harm." It was wisdom to humor them, it would be folly to give in to their demands.

When he assumed his duties as Pensionary of Holland, the Republic was at war with England. A conflict between the two naval powers had threatened for several years. British jealousy of Holland's flourishing carrying trade, quarrels about fishing rights in English waters, the memory of the Amboina executions, the battle of the Downs which violated English sovereignty, had created bad blood against the Republic and turned the name Dutch into a term of abuse. King Charles I had so many troubles to cope with at home that he lacked both the means and the power to teach these Dutch merchants a lesson. The rising power of the Prince of Orange had even persuaded him to marry his daughter Mary to Prince Frederick Henry's son, young William II. But that dynastic tie was no guarantee for the maintenance of peace after the downfall of the House of Stuart.

Three times in succession the two naval powers went to war against each other during the pensionaryship of Jan de

Witt. These were commercial conflicts between rivals. The Dutch championed the unrestricted freedom of the seas, the English their absolute sovereignty over their home waters; the Dutch wanted free trade in Europe, the English sought to cut down the freight-carrying activities of their rivals by protectionist measures. The English Parliament issued in 1681 the Navigation Act, which forbade the importation of foreign goods in other than English ships or in ships from the country of origin. It declared the carrying trade between England and her colonies to be a monopoly of the English merchant marine. And it prohibited foreigners from selling in the English market any fish they had illegally caught in English waters.

The Hollanders also championed their right to trade as neutrals with any belligerent in time of war, and the English theirs to hold up neutral vessels on the high seas and search them for contraband. Yet it was a mere breach of international etiquette that brought on the war: the English demanded that the Dutch should salute their flag in English waters in recognition of England's sovereignty. Admiral Tromp, sent out to sea to protect Dutch merchantmen against search, met Admiral Blake in the Channel, and the former's refusal to salute, or his tardiness in courtesy, led to the first exchange of shots.

The victory at sea shuttled back and forth between the enemy fleets. While the decision was hanging in the balance, Cromwell became Protector and De Witt Pensionary. The former did not favor the elimination of the Republic from the concert of Europe, for its defeat would strengthen the continental power of France. England was fighting a potential friend for the benefit of her worst enemy. Better make peace, he reasoned, with the Dutch Republic, which could serve England's cause better as her ally.

The peace treaty was signed at Westminster in April, 1654. The United Provinces were to pay an indemnity for the

Amboina murders; Dutch ships would salute the English flag in English waters; and the Stuarts, who had found refuge on Dutch soil, would be expelled from the Republic.

That last condition was conceded by De Witt and his party without the slightest demur. The royal uncle of the Prince of Orange was no friend of theirs and it did not cause them any heartbreak to refuse him asylum. Cromwell had demanded a pledge from the States-General that they would exclude forever the Prince of Orange from the stadtholderate and the chief command of their army. He withdrew that condition in return for the expulsion of the Stuarts and a promise on the part of Holland alone never again to entrust either function to a Prince of Orange.

De Witt was bitterly attacked in the States-General for this act of ingratitude to the House of Orange. The Pensionary argued, however, that Holland, as a sovereign state, was not accountable to the States-General for its choice of a stadtholder or its abolition of that office. But though he was able to refute his critics with legalistic arguments, he could not appease the wrath of the Orangist masses. The Act of Seclusion, as Holland's pact with Cromwell was called, remained a thorn in the flesh of the prince's followers. It was a cause of disharmony within Holland itself, where not all the cities had voted in its favor; it wrought disruption in the high command of the federal fleet, as Cornelis Tromp, the son of Marten, a stanch Orangist, refused to share responsibility with Michiel de Ruyter, who loyally stood by the States of Holland.

For the present, however, the issue between the two parties had only theoretical value, since the prince was still a little boy incapable of service in either office. The opposition against the act would gather force when its repeal could be translated into actual reappointment of the prince to the honors held by his ancestors. In the meantime, De Witt stood his ground without serious challenge from any quarter.

The Treaty of Westminster did not inaugurate an era of peace. The Republic was still at war with Portugal, and in the late fifties it became involved in a conflict between Sweden and Denmark. It intervened in the interests of Amsterdam, or—to be more explicit—Amsterdam forced Holland to involve the Republic in the Baltic quarrel. For just as Holland, on the strength of her predominant position in the Union, imposed her will on the other provinces, even so Amsterdam would dictate to the States of Holland and thwart De Witt's policies if they did not suit the city's interests. De Witt had successfully protected Danzig against the expansionist ambitions of Charles X of Sweden and concluded with the latter a satisfactory treaty at Elbing. But Amsterdam was not pleased with this solution, which let off the Swedish conqueror much too easily. He should be taught a lesson that he would not forget. The Treaty of Elbing, the city feared, would not stop him but would encourage him.

Charles X soon proved that Amsterdam was not mistaken. In the winter of 1657 he crossed the frozen Belt, invaded Denmark, and forced King Frederick III to sign the peace treaty of Roskilde. This placed Sweden in sole control of the Sound. Amsterdam's Baltic trade was in peril, and the city demanded that the Union should go to Denmark's aid. De Witt was not blind to the danger that threatened Holland's commerce. But Sweden was allied with England and France. Could he take the risk of antagonizing those two powers for the sake of thwarting Sweden's conquests, detrimental though these were to Amsterdam's trade?

The resumption of the war against Denmark by Charles X left him no choice. He had to act and acted promptly. A fleet was dispatched to the Sound, a crushing defeat delivered to the Swedes, Copenhagen relieved; and together with England and France, whom De Witt had persuaded to act with the Republic as mediators, a settlement was drawn up which Denmark signed voluntarily and which Sweden was forced to accept under pressure of Admiral de Ruyter's naval forces.

De Witt had maneuvered with great skill. He had thwarted Sweden, relieved Denmark, safeguarded Amsterdam's navigation through the Sound, and had managed to do all this in conjunction with the two powers that Sweden regarded as her allies. Amsterdam alone was dissatisfied. It had counted on a worse defeat for Sweden, but if De Witt had tried to play Amsterdam's game, he would have had to play it alone, and against, instead of together with, France and England.

The same year in which De Witt scored this diplomatic triumph saw the restoration of the Stuarts in England. King Charles II passed through The Hague on his way to London and was received with great ceremony by both the States-General and the States of Holland. The shipping interests in Holland were looking forward to a reversal of Cromwell's protectionist policy and improved relations with their rival across the North Sea. But the Navigation Act was not repealed, and the House of Commons, early in 1661, passed a bill that forbade all fishing by foreigners within a ten-mile limit from the British coast.

It was as colonial powers, however, that the two countries clashed. The king's brother James, Duke of York, utilized the people's animosity against the Dutch for his own ambitious ends. He had a large interest in the Royal African Company. A fleet equipped by this company seized, early in 1664, the Dutch factory at Cabo Corso on the Gold Coast, and in September of that same year an English fleet forced Director General Stuyvesant to surrender the colony of New Netherland which he had ruled for the Dutch West India Company since 1647. The Republic could not suffer these indignities lying down. The States-General dispatched their fleet under De Ruyter to the African coast, and as soon as the news of his mission reached London, the English government began hostilities in Europe. It declared war on the Dutch on March 4, 1665.

The first engagement between the two fleets ended disastrously for the Dutch. Their admiral, Jacob van Wassenaar-Obdam, was an army officer without naval experience. He belonged to the nobility of Holland, and had been chosen to head the navy not on account of special military ability but to reward the class to which he belonged for its support of the administration. His flagship blew up in the fray, and it was only owing to the skill of vice-admirals Cornelis Tromp and Johan Evertsen that the larger part of the fleet was brought safely into port. They had lost sixteen out of one hundred ships and two thousand of their twenty thousand men had lost their lives.

As soon as De Ruyter had returned from his mission to the Gold Coast and America, he was appointed commander in chief of the navy. It was the second time that the States, at a perilous juncture, turned to De Ruyter in their need. In the first war with England, the States of Zeeland, his native province, offered him the command over their contingent of the federal fleet. He refused, and stood by his refusal until their appeal to his patriotism made him yield. But he yielded reluctantly and on condition that his appointment should be for one voyage only.

For more than thirty years he had sailed the seven seas and shared the dangers of that adventurous life with daredevil crews who gloried in the tradition of the Sea Beggars. It was not cowardice that made him hesitate to accept command over the Zeeland squadron. He wavered because he knew that with these gangs of brave but undisciplined roughnecks a systematic naval war could not be waged. Raiding the enemy's coasts had been their pastime for generations; they had no conception of naval warfare that left the land untouched. And that was the kind of war that De Ruyter would have to wage against the English. For the freedom of the seas was in jeopardy. The Dutch Republic had to safeguard the routes of its overseas trade, and this could not be done by pillaging on land.

The British fleet had been unified under the command of military men schooled in the iron discipline of Cromwell's army. There was no centralized authority in the Dutch navy. Local and provincial pride thwarted all attempts at unification. There were five admiralties, each jealous of the others, and none possessing a navy worth the name. In case of war they would requisition armed merchantmen from various shipowners and combine them into a squadron. Thus, in 1640, De Ruyter, for the first time in his sea career, served the States of Zeeland on a ship that the latter had hired from her owner. With three other ships he was sent to the aid of the Portuguese, who had revolted against Spain. It was an ill-fated expedition. De Ruyter returned from it with no ambition to enter the service of the States for good. He bought with his savings the ship *Salamander,* and carried freight to and from the West Indies and the coast of North Africa until, in 1651, he decided to settle down to domesticity and peace.

But the Republic could not afford to let a man of his proved ability rest on his laurels. The reverses suffered by the Dutch navy in the first war with England were due to the deplorable conditions in the fleet, which De Ruyter exposed in his reports to the rulers at The Hague. The States of Holland, impressed by his foresight and intelligent criticism, offered him the vice-admiralty of Amsterdam. He declined, but was persuaded by Jan de Witt to reconsider and accept.

That was in 1655. It was the beginning of his ascent to glory. Until then he had been one among a host of daring captains who combined privateering with trading. From 1655 on he was one of a small number of vice-admirals, and as commander of the admiralty of Amsterdam he was the first among his equals. Backed by the authority of Jan de Witt, who himself went to sea with the fleet more than once, he created order out of chaos.

He built up a navy that no longer needed to rely on armed merchantmen for reinforcement; he saw to it that the new men-of-war were built all of one type so that replacements and repairs could be obtained without delay from the stores and arsenals on land; he made up for the shortage of trained officers by the formation of a professional cadre, and had the fleet on extended expeditions accompanied by supply ships.

Until De Ruyter took command for the admiralty of Amsterdam the captains were responsible for the victualing of their own ships, and the grafters among them enriched themselves at the expense of their crews, charging the admiralty for more and better food than they actually bought. De Ruyter insisted on the establishment of an efficient supply and rationing system. Thus the makeshift conglomeration of privateering merchantmen was superseded by a disciplined and firmly organized battle fleet, whose striking power was demonstrated in the famous Four Days' Battle, fought between North Foreland and Dunkirk in the middle of June, 1666.

Monck and Rupert, who commanded the English fleet, had their revenge less than two months later. They scored a decisive victory owing to a tactical blunder of Cornelis Tromp; but De Ruyter succeeded in saving his fleet from destruction by withdrawing under the protection of the Zeeland coast. Tromp was accused by De Ruyter of desertion, and deprived of his command by the States of Holland.

Meanwhile France had come to the aid of the Dutch Republic, or—to be more exact—had declared war on England as an ally of the States-General. For the military support King Louis XIV gave the Dutch was negligible. His aim was not to save the United Provinces from defeat but to prevent them from coming to terms with the English on the basis of an alliance against France. For Louis XIV had his eye on the Spanish Netherlands, and he foresaw that, since the Republic was not anxious to have France as a neighbor and England would scarcely be pleased at seeing Antwerp fall into French hands, his invasion of that territory would meet with opposition from the two sea powers. Louis XIV would rather help the Dutch fight the English than see the two enemies reconciled and in league against himself.

Charles II tried to persuade the States-General to conclude a separate peace, but this time they stood by their French ally. Louis XIV hardly deserved such loyalty. Before the negotiations were opened at Breda, he promised Charles II that he would stay out of the war during 1667, if the latter did not undertake any hostile action against France. And as soon as the deliberations were under way, the French king announced his claims to the Spanish Netherlands, which were promptly invaded by a French army.

These events did not tend to produce the right atmosphere for the conduct of peace negotiations. While the delegates at Breda were talking and deliberating to little purpose, De Witt decided on a bold move that was calculated to make the British more amenable. De Ruyter sailed to the Thames with a fleet of over eighty ships. He occupied the mouth with his main force, and sent Admiral Joseph van Ghent, who had succeeded Cornelis Tromp, up the Medway. He broke through the chain with which the river had been blocked, destroyed several English men-of-war, captured others including the flagship *Royal Charles,* and created a panic in London.

The shock to English prestige had its effect on the negotiations at Breda. Five weeks later peace was concluded (July 31, 1667). The Navigation Act was modified, and commercial advantages were conceded. New Netherland remained in British hands, but in return the Dutch retained Surinam, which they had taken from the English.

The French, meanwhile, had occupied part of the southern Netherlands without much resistance from the Spanish.

De Witt had neither the intention nor the means to go to war against France. But he understood the diplomatic game on the European chessboard. He found an expert partner in Sir William Temple, the British ambassador at The Hague. And the Swedish ambassador Dohna, who shared their anti-French bias, was easily persuaded by the promise of subsidies to make common cause with the two naval powers. On January 26, 1668 they concluded the Triple Alliance for the purpose of mediating between France and Spain.

Louis XIV, in the face of this coalition, did not try to force the issue. He could bide his time, make a show of moderation, and strike again as soon as the threefold partnership, which he knew to be precarious, began to disintegrate. He accepted its mediation with apparent good grace, and by the Treaty of Aix-la-Chapelle agreed to withdraw his troops from the Franche-Comté, though not from the frontier towns in the Spanish Netherlands.

Jan de Witt had reached the zenith of his power. He wielded the baton in the concert of Europe. But his very successes bore the seeds of his destruction. Conscious of his skill, and overconfident through fortune's persistent favor, he scorned, or failed to see, the forebodings of the gathering storm. Both at home and abroad the forces he had antagonized were banding together to take their vengeance and strike him down at the first opportunity.

At home the Orangists were agitating with increasing insistence as the young Prince of Orange approached his majority. De Witt thought he could weather that storm by making concessions. He had young William declared "Child of State," with the consent of the boy's grandmother Amalia, the widow of Prince Frederick Henry. The title gave his well-wishers for a time an illusion of preferment for their favorite, but they soon realized that the sound had cheated them out of the substance. A commission, of which De Witt himself was a member, was entrusted with the education of the "Child of State," but to the Orangists this was not half enough and to the enemies of the dynasty it seemed an alarming omen of its future restoration. To forestall that calamity, they forced through the assembly of the States of Holland, not with the full approval of De Witt, a measure that they were pleased to call "Eternal Edict," a name whose unintended irony would soon become apparent in the light of subsequent events. It declared the stadtholderate in Holland abolished forever, and the majority who passed it resolved in addition that the other provinces should be invited to declare that no stadtholder could ever be commander in chief of either the army or the navy. The measure was carried in the States-General, but with only a bare majority, three of the seven provinces voting against it. Its passage could hardly be construed as a victory for De Witt's party. This paper bar against the restoration of the prince to the full power possessed by his father and grandfather gave them no sense of security, and its chief effect was increased bitterness among the Orangists and hatred of all that De Witt stood for.

The Republic's foreign relations were also taking a turn for the worse. Pieter de Groot, who was ambassador at Paris, sent warning upon warning to De Witt that Louis XIV was preparing for war against the Republic, and that England would fight on his side. The King of France had succeeded in breaking the Triple Alliance, but De Witt, though advised by his ambassadors of the mischief that was brewing, refused to believe that Charles II would play him false. Being himself a man of scrupulous integrity, he put a naïve trust, incomprehensible in a statesman of that age, in the honesty of others.

Charles II was detached from the Triple Alliance by the persuasion of his favorite sister Henrietta, Duchess of Orléans, whom the King of France employed as his emissary. Her arguments for a change of policy were buttressed by a bribe of three million francs a year and the promise of a foothold on the Isle of Walcheren. She was a clever and adroit advocate for the cause in which she was employed. War between France and the Dutch Republic being inevitable, only three courses were open to her brother, she explained to Charles. He might remain neutral, but the maintenance of neutrality was a precarious and thankless task, as precarious as the role of a belligerent, and less profitable than that of a victorious one. Much better to take sides, and England's interest demanded that he side with Louis XIV against the Dutch. For the Republic was the real rival of England. France, it is true, was a domineering, arrogant and ambitious power, but her interests did not clash with those of England in the way that those of the Dutch did.

"It is true," she wrote in one of her letters to Charles, "that by establishing your dominion on the ruins of that of Holland you will also contribute towards increasing that of the King of France, who aspires perhaps not less than yourself to becoming supreme in commerce. But the situation of your kingdom, the number, the extent, and the order of your ports, which are suitable for the biggest vessels, the natural disposition of your subjects and the convenience you possess for building vessels remarkable for the manner of their construction and their power of endurance are advantages which France cannot possess."

But those advantages were actually possessed by the Dutch, and for that reason Holland was the more dangerous rival, which had to be crushed before England could build a colonial empire. Charles was not unwilling to be convinced. The disgrace of the Medway incident and the peace of Breda rankled in his memory. Hatred of the Dutch and the prospect of taking revenge upon them weakened his distrust of the King of France. And so the secret treaty of Dover was signed on the last day of the year 1670, by which Charles agreed to declare war upon Holland when called upon to do so by King Louis.

French diplomacy, meanwhile, was also mustering allies that could attack the Dutch Republic from the east. Two powerful prelates of Germany aligned themselves with France against the United Provinces. One was the Bishop of Münster, who laid claim to certain territory under the rule of the States-General, the other was the Archbishop of Cologne. The latter was a Bavarian prince with strong pro-French leanings. He was also Bishop of Liége, and as such he allowed the King of France free passage for his armies across his diocese when the invasion of the Republic should begin.

Charles II was the first to declare war, on March 28, 1672. Louis XIV followed suit on April 6. Events moved swiftly after that. A French army of 120,000 men poured through the territory of the Bishop of Liége into Brabant and from there into the provinces of Gelderland and Utrecht, and the two German bishops attacked the Republic from the east. The States of Holland, under pressure of the aroused populace, proposed the appointment for one year of the Prince of Orange as commander in chief of the army. The proposal was carried over the opposition of De Witt. In his twenty-first year William III was called to the superhuman task of opposing, with a field force of four thousand badly trained and undisciplined men, the best army in Europe, led by generals, such as Condé, Turenne, Luxembourg, who had mastered the art of war through lifelong experience. The prince withdrew with his hopelessly outnumbered troops behind the Dutch waterline. The States of Zeeland appointed him stadtholder, those of Holland repealed the Eternal Edict—six years after its eternity had been proclaimed—and restored, at the motion of Amsterdam, the stadtholderate in favor of the Prince of Orange. And on July 8, 1672, the States-General appointed him commander in chief of both army and navy. De Witt's "Child of State" had become, overnight, master of state.

The Pensionary bowed to the inevitable and handed in his

resignation. He realized that the people, in their extreme peril, wanted a scapegoat, and that they would avenge their country's plight on him. And not on him only: his brother Cornelis would have to suffer with him. The latter had been jailed on a trumped-up charge that he had plotted to murder the prince. Jan de Witt escaped an attempt on his life. Cornelis was put to the torture, but steadfastly maintained his innocence. Since no confession of guilt could be extorted from him, his judges condemned him to banishment and loss of all his offices. The same day on which sentence was pronounced a fake message, purporting to come from Cornelis in prison, summoned Jan de Witt to his brother's cell. While he was there, an angry crowd gathered in front of the jail; the troops that stood guard at the gate were ordered away by the executive committee of the States of Holland, on the pretext that riotous peasants were on the march against The Hague and had to be stopped before they reached the city. A civic guard was the only protection that remained. But the mob instinctively knew, or its ringleaders had been assured, that the civic guard would only put up a token resistance. The jail was stormed, the brothers struck down with rifle butts, dragged down the stairs, and butchered in the street outside in a revolting access of mass fury.

It was not the rabble of The Hague that was guilty of this atrocity. Among the ringleaders were a banker and a goldsmith. The Reverend Simonides, of the Dutch Reformed Church, referred to the murder from the pulpit, the next day, as an act of divine vengeance, and Admiral Cornelis Tromp recommended one of the ringleaders afterward for preferment. The massacre was an act of perverted patriotism in which members of all classes participated. Cherishing the memory of Prince William I, who had been martyred for Dutch liberty, the Calvinists saw in the House of Orange the cornerstone of the Republic. De Witt and his fellow builders of what they called True Freedom had rejected the cornerstone, and the structure, in consequence, collapsed when storms from the west, south, and east fell upon it. By his wicked exclusion of the prince from all offices, De Witt had prepared the way for the country's downfall. Only the third Prince William, they knew, could save it. Their intense hatred of De Witt was a corollary of their idolatrous love of the House of Orange. He had outraged that love, and the Republic's present plight, which their instinct told them could not have come about under the guardianship of the House of Orange, made them fall, like frightened beasts of prey, upon the man they held to blame for their peril. Thus perished one of Holland's noblest and greatest statesmen, who had served his country, according to his conception of what was best for it, with strict integrity and singular devotion.

CHAPTER VII

The French Menace

THAT DAY of August 25, 1672, was the blackest in the blackest year of the Republic's history. That the country survived and came out of the ordeal unscathed seems a miracle, the more miraculous because its salvation was achieved under the leadership of a young man barely out of his teens, who had no experience of either war or diplomacy.

Prince William III had been trained in a hard school. As Child of State he was surrounded by men who distrusted him and were determined to prevent his rise to power. He had learned at an early age, in self-defense, to keep his own counsel. Under an outwardly austere and imperturbable demeanor burned a fiery, passionate nature. His health was delicate, but by strength of will he forced his feeble frame to endure the hardships of war and the fatigue of protracted deliberations in the council room. He was utterly fearless and never deigned to take precautions against the hazards of the battlefield or the plots of assassins. He was a master of statecraft, and seemed to know by instinct, at twenty-one, what others only learned by years of experience. When he assumed command of the federal army, he was a novice in the military profession. Yet, confronted on the battlefield by opponents who were among the greatest generals of the age, he stood his ground not without honor, though he never scored a decisive victory. As a strategist he was at his best in the hour of frustration. Never losing his composure or control of all his faculties, he rallied his forces with surprising skill and rapidity, and repaired the danger of defeat before the enemy could turn it into disaster.

He was not left to fight the Republic's battles alone. In 1673 the emperor and Spain promised aid, Spain on condition that France was to be repelled within the frontiers established by the Treaty of the Pyrenees. Much had changed in the course of one generation. The Hapsburgs, enemies in the forties, had become allies, and France, then aiding the Republic against Spain, was now their common foe. It was a sad demonstration of the wickedness and absurdity of wars undertaken for no better reason than a sovereign's desire for aggrandizement of his realm. Hugo Grotius, in his *De Jure Belli ac Pacis* (1625), had denied a sovereign prince's right to wage war for the satisfaction of his territorial ambitions, and had branded the instigator of such a war a criminal under international law deserving to be punished by international co-operation. But his wisdom was far ahead of his time. The practice of that age disregarded his teaching and built its international relations upon alliances that had to resort to war for the maintenance of a vacillating balance of power.

The water citadel of Holland was invaded when a severe winter frost gave the French passage across the ice. But a sudden thaw forced the invaders to withdraw. The city of Groningen successfully withstood the armies of the two episcopal warlords, Münster and Cologne, and saved by its firmness the province of Friesland from being overrun by the enemy. The rest of the country fell prey to the attackers. But Prince William, ably assisted by his field marshal, Count von Waldeck, undertook a bold march into the Rhineland and, reinforced by imperial troops, captured Bonn by surprise. The Archbishop of Cologne had ceded that city to Louis XIV as a supply base, and here the king had amassed large stores of ordnance and ammunition purchased from Amsterdam merchants whose lust for private gain was stronger than their love of country. The French armies, severed from their life line, withdrew from Dutch territory, and the two German prelates, for lack of French support, evacuated the eastern provinces and made peace with the Republic. By the end of 1673 the country was free of invaders.

At sea, De Ruyter, reconciled with Tromp through Prince William's mediation, had been equally successful. Although one-third of his fleet was laid up in 1673 because the crews were needed to help the army stem the onrush of the French invaders, he was able to defeat the combined naval forces of the French and the British. No landing on Holland's coast was attempted. In her greatest peril, De Ruyter's navy prevented invasion from the sea.

The province, in gratitude for so narrow an escape from disaster, declared the stadtholderate hereditary in the male line; Zeeland, Utrecht, Gelderland, and Overijsel followed suit; and the States-General made the prince hereditary commander in chief of the federal army and navy. If he had seized sovereign power none would have opposed him. But he was satisfied with the influence he wielded through the right that was given him to fill vacancies in the municipal governments. He was often unscrupulous in the choice of his appointees. Slavish subservience to his orders was to him the best recommendation. Courageous and independent himself, he had little use for men of courage and independent character. The caliber of the oligarchy deteriorated as a result, a change whose fatal consequences were to become apparent in the next century.

The prince was concerned with immediate ends, and employed the tools that served the needs of the moment. He did not aspire to greater honor for himself within the Republic, but sought greater power for the Republic on the Continent. For his mind was surveying a vaster field than the limited territory of the Union. There would be no enduring safety for the United Provinces, he realized, unless France were balked for good in her desire for expansion. To isolate her and encircle her with a ring of allies sworn to aid one another in holding her within bounds was the mission that he set himself.

He won the first round in the diplomatic battle when he concluded peace with England. The war was not popular over there. The Protestant subjects of Charles II saw more shame than profit in the alliance with His Catholic Majesty against the Protestant Republic. King Charles yielded to the rising demand for peace. He came to terms with the Dutch by the Treaty of Westminster, on February 19, 1674. The Republic undertook to pay within three years a war indemnity of two million guilders; to recognize British sovereignty in British waters on condition that the Dutch herring fleet should have free fishing there; and to surrender again New Netherland, which their fleet had retaken. But they did not concede England's right to search neutral vessels for contraband, and the English did not press that point, for a very good reason. Since Holland's war with France continued, the Dutch might turn that two-edged weapon against the merchant fleet of neutral England.

France was now isolated and opposed by a coalition of the Hapsburg powers and the Republic, which were presently joined by Brandenburg and Denmark. But French diplomacy succeeded in encircling the allies in their turn with a still wider ring of French supporters: Sweden, Poland, Turkey. There was little cohesion between the enemies of France. The Spanish and imperial generals were unwilling to cede the supreme command of the allied armies to Prince William and thwarted, rather than supported, his daring attempts to come to battle with the French. The war dragged on without yielding him any victories. His only triumphs were masterly escapes from defeat. At sea the Dutch did not fare any better. De Ruyter was sent to the Mediterranean to help the Spanish quell a revolt in Messina fomented by

French intrigue. He objected to sailing with a fleet inadequately equipped. For the States, in their shortsightedness, had failed to maintain the navy's wartime efficiency after the peace with England had been signed. Had he lost his courage in his old age, one of the merchant rulers had the impudence to ask him? "Where the States will risk their flag, I will risk my life," was his dignified answer. His dead body returned from that expedition and was buried on March 18, 1677 in the New Church at Amsterdam.

The prince's popularity suffered a setback as a result of these reverses. The cost of the war rose to alarming heights. The merchants of Holland complained of heavy losses due to English competition in the ports of France and to the piracy of Dunkirk privateers. Early in 1676 French and Dutch delegates met at Nijmegen to discuss terms of peace, and toward the end of that year they were joined by envoys of Spain and the emperor, who were afraid that the Republic would conclude a separate peace with France. It was, indeed, King Louis' intention to detach the States-General from their Hapsburg allies. In 1672 he had hoped through the destruction of the Republic to conquer the Spanish Netherlands. Now, five years later, he reverted to the policy of Richelieu, who, in the forties, had striven for a partition of that coveted territory between France and the United Provinces. It was less costly to attain his aim by an amicable arrangement with the Dutch. The tax-burdened citizens of Holland, he hoped, would bring pressure to bear upon the States-General in favor of a speedy peace. And the latter would yield, no doubt, if the terms he offered were generous.

But the prince was adamant. He would not consent to a separate peace. The war should be carried on until France was defeated. A sudden change in English policy seemed to justify his obstinacy. Charles II invited him to come to London and offered him the Princess Mary, daughter of the Duke of York, in marriage. William brought her home as his wife, fully confident that this convincing token of British good will and support would silence the clamor for peace. But his English marriage was unpopular in Holland. The States distrusted Charles II. The king soon gave proof, to William's distress, of his unreliability. King Louis knew him better than did his nephew. A handsome French bribe was sufficient to prevent all his promises of military aid from being honored. Louis' armies, meanwhile, made rapid progress in Flanders. Betrayed by England, and feebly supported by Spain, the States-General had no choice but to accept the French king's not ungenerous terms. France withdrew from her most advanced conquests in the Spanish Netherlands, retaining chiefly parts of the Walloon provinces along the French frontier; allowed the Dutch to retain Maastricht; and offered them a highly favorable trade agreement. This, and the maintenance of a buffer state between the Republic and France, were the chief gains that the envoys of the States-General brought home from Nijmegen.

Prince William's continental policy seemed shattered beyond repair. The States-General, by concluding a separate peace, had alienated their friends across the Rhine. In their anxiety to safeguard the Union's southern border, they gave scant thought to the buttressing of their eastern front. Brandenburg, Denmark, and Austria were left to disentangle themselves from the war as best they could. The first of these, now facing Sweden alone, found security in an alliance with France, and the emperor, harassed by the Turks, was not likely to lend his support a second time to so faithless an ally. The Dutch had bought a precarious and temporary safety at a very high price. They had paid for it with Prince William's anti-French coalition.

It seemed a hopeless undertaking to rebuild the structure, the more so since the dissension over the peace within the Republic had estranged the prince from his late supporters in Holland. Amsterdam was now in the vanguard of the opposition. The old distrust of the House of Orange was revived, and all attempts of the prince to stem a new French invasion of Flanders in 1683 were thwarted by the city's stubborn refusal to vote appropriations for the levying of troops. The unbridled language of the prince, who openly accused the Amsterdam rulers of collusion with the French ambassador, did not make the opposition more amenable. It even stiffened when Louis XIV declared his willingness to arrange a truce. This move won a majority for the antiwar party in the States-General. For Friesland, whose stadtholder Henry Casimir was jealous of his famous cousin, together with Zeeland and Overijsel, aligned themselves with Holland against the Prince. Spain was forced, under a twenty-year truce, to cede Luxemburg to France, and the emperor, made helpless by the Turkish menace, ratified the treaty, leaving Strassburg, which the French had seized in 1681, in King Louis' hands.

Prince William found himself beaten a second time by a selfish and shortsighted oligarchy which did not see that the Republic's safety was not a thing apart but intimately bound up with the safety of the Continent from French domination. But at the moment of his deepest despair he received support from an unexpected quarter. The King of France himself brought the most convincing proof of the reality of the menace against which William had warned the States-General in vain. His revocation of the Edict of Nantes, in 1685, opened the eyes of the politically blind to the king's real aims. The accounts of the Huguenot fugitives who fled to the Republic by the tens of thousands left no doubt in Dutch minds that His Catholic Majesty was launched on a crusade against Protestantism.

The Elector of Brandenburg, the principal Protestant state of the empire, and his old enemy Sweden, together with a number of smaller Rhenish states, now joined the Republic to uphold the treaties of Westphalia and Nijmegen against the aggression of France; and the Catholic Hapsburgs of Spain and Austria made common cause with this Protestant alignment to pay off old scores with their hereditary enemy. This rallying of the Protestants around the banner raised by Prince William received additional impetus from reports of political changes in England. King Charles II had died in 1685 and his Catholic brother James, Duke of York, had succeeded him. Common zeal for their Protestant faith reunited political enemies. Amsterdam's burgomasters effected a reconciliation with the prince, his cousin Henry Casimir promised him loyal support, and d'Avaux, the French ambassador, lamented the passing of the days when he found good fishing in the troubled waters of the Republic's domestic politics.

William's improved relations with Amsterdam came at an opportune moment. The conflict between James II and his Protestant subjects had come to a head with the birth of a male heir to the throne. William was invited by a group of prominent Englishmen to come to England with an army and help the people rise against their king. He could not have ventured on such a course without the backing of Amsterdam and the States-General. Both favored the expedition. On November 14 he landed in Torbay. James, deserted by all, fled to France. And on February 13, 1689 a convention, summoned by William for the occasion, declared the throne vacant and offered the crown to William and Mary.

England had been the missing link in the chain with which the Prince of Orange hoped to encircle and restrain France. Now the ring was closed and Louis faced a formidable coalition of nearly all Europe. But numbers of allies did not make for efficient use of strength. The war with France dragged on for years and ended in a stalemate. By the peace treaty of Ryswick, Louis evacuated Luxemburg and all his conquests in the Spanish Netherlands and offered the Republic a favorable commercial treaty; while Spain allowed the Dutch to garrison a series of fortresses along the southern frontier of her Netherlands territories.

The treaty brought not a cessation but only a suspension of hostilities. Louis offered easy peace terms because he had reason to expect that the prize which he had vainly tried to win by means of costly wars would fall to him without military effort in a game of diplomacy. King Charles II of Spain was expected to die before long. Louis was anxious to come to terms with the two maritime powers and settle with them the partition of the Spanish Empire. Prince William was not averse to such a scheme so long as the disposal of other people's territories did not make France a next-door neighbor of the Republic. The statesmen in Madrid, however, were determined to save the unity of the realm, at whatever cost; and believing that the King of France had the power to maintain it, they persuaded King Charles to will all his dominions to Louis' second grandson, Philip of Anjou. He died a month later, on November 1, 1700, and early next year French troops marched into the Spanish Netherlands to occupy them for the new king.

The menace that had obsessed the statesmen at The Hague for more than half a century had suddenly become a reality: the Republic had France for its neighbor. For it was obvious that Philip V had given his grandfather a free hand in the Netherlands. They had become, to all intents and purposes, an outlying province of France.

Prince William and Anthony Heinsius, the Pensionary of Holland, set to work at once to repair the dilapidated Grand Alliance. A treaty was signed at The Hague between the emperor and the maritime powers under which the signatories agreed that the Italian possessions of Spain should fall to Austria, the Spanish Netherlands should be maintained as a buffer state between France and the Republic, and the maritime powers would retain any conquests they might make in the West Indies.

Heinsius had little difficulty in carrying the States-General along with him in the pursuit of this policy. The danger of sharing their southern frontier with France took the wind out of the antiwar party's sails. In England there was stronger opposition. But the French king, again, played into William's hands. James II died in France on September 6, 1701, and Louis, who by the peace of Ryswick had recognized William as King of England and Mary's sister Anne as his heir, promptly acknowledged the Prince of Wales as King James III. This duplicity dispelled all opposition and William obtained the needed war supplies and troops without difficulty.

But in the midst of feverish preparations for war the king-stadtholder suddenly died. His will had overtaxed his strength. A riding accident gave to his undermined system a shock from which he was not able to recover. He was the last Prince of Orange directly descended from William the Silent. That noble line passed out in glory. The first William had been outlawed and murdered by order of the King of Spain. The third, as leader of the Republic the other had founded, headed, at the time of his death, a European coalition that would decide the partition of the decayed Spanish Empire. The mills of God grind slowly, but they grind exceeding small.

William had appointed as his heir the young stadtholder of Friesland and Groningen, John William Friso, the son of Henry Casimir. He was but fourteen years of age, and although the five other provinces had declared the stadtholderate hereditary, they ignored his right to the succession on account of his youth. Anthony Heinsius, as Pensionary of Holland, became the political leader of the Republic.

In the treaty concluded at The Hague the signatories did not refer to the succession in Spain, as if they had no intention of ousting King Philip V from the throne. But under pressure from England and the emperor, the States-General were persuaded to revise their war aims with regard to the Spanish succession. The allies, it was decided, would support the claims of the Archduke Charles, the emperor's youngest son, to the Spanish throne. Escorted by a fleet of the two maritime powers the Austrian pretender landed in Catalonia and carried the war into the peninsula. The fleet subsequently captured Gibraltar and Minorca, but the Dutch at home, alarmed by the rising cost of the war and forced to concentrate all their efforts on the campaigns in the Spanish Netherlands, began to neglect the upkeep of the fleet, withdrew their squadron from the Mediterranean, and left the English in sole possession of Gibraltar.

The States-General had consented to the arrangement that made John Churchill, Earl of Marlborough, commander in chief of the Dutch and British armies, on condition, however, that he should consult their civilian deputies as to the use to which he would put their forces. The imperial armies were headed by Prince Eugene of Savoy. Both men were brilliant strategists and far superior to their French opponents. The cautious Dutch deputies irked Marlborough's patience beyond endurance, and he claimed, not unjustly perhaps, that but for their obstinacy, he could have finished the war much sooner. But the Dutch could hardly be blamed for not placing confidence equal to his own in his yet unproven military genius, and the risks he took, if unsuccessful, would have been much more disastrous to the Republic, so close to the scene of action, than to England safely ensconced behind her sea barrier.

The outcome of his battles proved his greatness, and gave him so preponderant a position in the Grand Alliance that he seemed on his way to becoming the arbiter of Europe's destinies. But a change in the domestic policies of England undermined his power. His wife fell out of favor with Queen Anne, the Whig ministry was supplanted by a Tory cabinet, and the new government, preferring British isolation to entanglement on the Continent, entered upon secret negotiations with France. Louis XIV had sued for peace in 1710, but had been rebuffed by the allies when he refused to accede to their demand that he help them expel his grandson from Spain. He admitted defeat, but would not sign away his honor. The political change in England brightened his hope of better terms. And another windfall dispelled his worst forebodings. The Emperor Joseph died suddenly in 1711, after a reign of five years, and was succeeded by his younger brother Charles, the pretender to the Spanish crown. England was not willing to help him restore the world empire of Charles V. The imperial and Spanish crowns were too many for one head. Since the power of France was broken by her latest reverses, it was safer to leave King Philip V in possession of his throne. England suspended all her military preparations, Marlborough was recalled, and delegates from the various belligerent powers met at Utrecht to make peace.

The States-General had to pay dearly for their former intransigence. Under pressure from Great Britain they had insisted on the ousting of King Philip with his grandfather's aid; now they had to resign themselves to leaving him undisturbed on his throne. And the terms they could obtain from France, now that the most humiliating condition was dropped, were worse for them instead of better. For as King Louis' bargaining power had risen, theirs had gone down. While the negotiations were in progress, the combined armies of the emperor and the Republic, no longer supported by the English, were badly defeated at Denain. They came to the peace table with diminished prestige and facing an enemy who, narrowly saved from destruction, would repay past humiliation with all the chicanery of which diplomacy is capable. "On traitera de la paix chez vous, pour vous, sans vous," said one of the French envoys to the Dutch delegation. The insult was the more grievous because it told the truth. The real negotiations were carried on between England and

France, and England's allies would have to sign on the dotted line.

There existed a secret pact between England and the Republic that dated from 1709. It embodied an engagement on England's part to help the States-General obtain the right to hold and to garrison a number of towns along the French frontier, a right that would give them not only a barrier against France but also economic control of the southern Netherlands. With that promise England had bribed the Dutch into rejecting Louis' peace offer by demanding from him the impossible. The Tory government was loath to stand by that agreement. For France refused to fulfill the conditions that England, in their secret negotiations, had stipulated for herself, unless the States-General were persuaded to waive their claim on English aid as promised under that Barrier Treaty. A bitter press campaign led by Jonathan Swift was launched in England against the scandalous provisions of the agreement with the Dutch, and against the States-General, which because of their unwillingness to sign such a waiver, were accused of trying to prolong the war in hope of bleeding England white. The British government repudiated the Barrier Treaty as prejudicial to British interests, since it would give the Republic extension of territory and greater economic strength; and the rulers at The Hague had to be satisfied with a substitute treaty which was much more favorable to France and shorn of the great privileges of taxation and trading that made the earlier pact so valuable to the Dutch. The only salvage from their diplomatic shipwreck was the promise of a right to garrison a limited number of frontier towns in the southern Netherlands. A promise, not the right itself. For England could not dispose of territory that belonged to the emperor, to whom Spain agreed, under the Treaty of Utrecht, to cede her Netherlands territories.

The Dutch, however, were furnished at Utrecht with one

effective argument for persuading the emperor to let them have their way. The treaty provided that the former Spanish possession, still occupied by Dutch and English troops, would not be handed over to him until he had satisfied the Dutch as to their Barrier. After the return of the Whigs to power in 1714, the English government did its best to reconcile the emperor and the States-General but made little headway in bringing the parties together. Even after a third Barrier Treaty had been concluded in November, 1715, between England, the emperor, and the Dutch Republic, the matter was not settled. The disputes continued until finally in October, 1718, a convention was effected that satisfied all concerned.

The Barrier was practically the only trophy that the United Provinces brought home from the war. The chief spoils fell to England: domination of the Mediterranean through her occupancy of Gibraltar and Minorca, extension of her North American territory at the expense of France, commercial advantages in South America. The Treaty of Utrecht laid the foundations of England's colonial and maritime greatness. It also marked the end of a period in Dutch history. The Republic's heyday was over, though its glory was to linger on, in the eighteenth century, as, with diminishing strength, it moved toward its setting.

CHAPTER VIII

The Golden Age

THE DUTCH call the century of Oldenbarnevelt, De Witt, and William III the Golden Age of the Netherlands. It was a small nation that under their leadership wrested its freedom from Spain and rose to political equality with France and England. The entire population of the Republic, around 1600, amounted to no more than 1,000,000, and 600,000 of these lived in the province of Holland, where most of its wealth, its talent, and its intellect were concentrated.

Foreigners were impressed and puzzled by the strange phenomenon of an upstart commonwealth run by merchants and asserting itself, in spite of its limited size, against long established monarchies. Travelers visited Holland to find an answer to the riddle. There were, of course, many contributory causes. Among these a very important one was the Republic's financial stability. The United Provinces were the only state in Europe that was solvent all through the century. Holland's credit abroad was so firmly established that she could borrow money cheaply. In 1668 the States-General refused a loan that was offered them at two and a half per cent. Sir William Temple, then ambassador at The Hague, wondered why King Charles II could not borrow money at six, if he put his finances in order and paid his creditors promptly.

The discrepancy between the rate of interest in England and that of the Republic was to the envious English an economic puzzle. It was due, no doubt, to the backwardness of

England as compared to the highly developed organization of commerce and finance in the Netherlands. The businessmen who ruled the country administered its affairs in a businesslike manner. Being unhampered by lack of funds, they could see to it that their army and navy were well and regularly paid; and well-paid fighting forces could be disciplined and relied upon. The Republic's successes in war were due, in no small measure, to a balanced budget.

That happy state of solvency was owing to the industry of the people and the wealth it produced. The herring fisheries, the carrying trade, the East and West India companies, the whaling industry, and all the numerous arts and crafts that flourished in the Republic were sources of prosperity and affluence. New industries were introduced by aliens who found a refuge in Holland and gave their energy and skill in return for her tolerant hospitality. The Huguenots especially and the refugees from the southern Netherlands contributed to the upswing of Holland's economic life. The many and various factories that they established made the Dutch the leading industrial nation of the world. Most of these immigrants settled in Amsterdam, but other cities with established industries were also benefited by this influx of skilled labor. The manufacture of linens was centered in Haarlem, Leyden was famous for its cloths, Delft for its potteries and breweries, Dordrecht for the linen thread that was spun there, Gouda for its cordage and clay pipes. But Amsterdam was Holland's industrial metropolis. Here all kinds of tapestry were made, here were mills for sawing timber, for the polishing of marble, for the cutting and polishing of diamonds, for the making of gunpowder; here were refineries for sugar, salt, cinnamon, camphor and other products from exotic lands. Here they made velvets, satins, and silks, gold and silver brocades, ribbons of all kinds, lace, paper, and many other articles of luxury which, said a contemporary English writer, sold twenty per cent cheaper than they did in France. In short, there was work for all hands. Everyone was employed, down to the lame and the gouty, said another observer, and even those who had arthritis in their hands did not sit idle.

James Howell, who visited Amsterdam in 1619, wrote to his father that it was a rare thing to meet with a beggar there, and a century later Lady Mary Wortley Montague observed the same in Rotterdam. Loafers and vagrants who refused to work were taken care of in reformatories. Amsterdam maintained a home for wayward girls which bore this inscription over the entrance:

FEAR NOT, I VENGE NO WRONG, BUT FORCE YOU TO BE GOOD.
HARD IS MY HAND, INDEED, BUT GENTLE IS MY MOOD.

In their care for the neglected child and the potential criminal the Dutch magistrates were pioneers.

Since most aliens settled in the cities, where labor was in greater demand than on the land, there was less mixture of races in the rural districts. Yet the Dutch country folk shared in the general prosperity. John Evelyn was told that many a farmer invested his savings in pictures because there was no land for sale: that had all been bought up by city capitalists. Scarcity of farm land stimulated the reclamation of lakes and pools. Jan Adriaenszoon Leechwater, a mill builder and hydraulic engineer, transformed many a wet spot of Holland into a fertile polder. His genius launched the campaign that was to culminate in our time in the drainage of the Zuider Zee. He wrote a chronicle of these activities, recording from year to year the pools reclaimed, the mills, workshops and town halls erected in the new polders, the new industries started where formerly was a waste of water.

The watery nature of the land made settlement in these new-made regions attractive. For no farmer was isolated on his polder property. A network of canals gave easy access to nearly every part, no matter how remote. In other countries transportation was expensive and increased the sale price of commodities; in Holland all freight was carried in barges that were pulled by a single horse. Even wealthy merchants built summer homes in the polders, and their presence among the rural population made the latter acquainted with the amenities of city life.

The foreign travelers who published their impressions of the Dutch Republic commented, without exception, on the freedom from servility among the lower classes. The anonymous author of *The Dutch Drawn to the Life* said the Dutch were all equal. There was no way of knowing the servant from the mistress. If your footman was saucy you had no right to cane him, which, to judge from his astonishment, was a common practice in England. The Frenchman De Parival, author of *Les Délices de la Hollande* (1665), confessed he had never seen such treatment of servants elsewhere, and Bentheim, a German, remarked that a threat to beat a domestic might get the master into trouble, as upon the servant's complaint he would have to answer for it in court.

Sir William Temple, commenting on the inconspicuous manner in which even the highest in the land appeared in public, ascribed to this self-restraint of the ruling class the common people's willingness to submit to their authority and to the heavy taxes that were levied on them. Jan de Witt was usually seen on foot and unattended, like any other burgher of The Hague, and the same was true of Vice-Admiral de Ruyter at Amsterdam.

The only vice, in fact, that Sir Thomas Overbury found among the Dutch was their love of drinking. Sir William Temple, who wrote half a century later, did not confirm that charge. According to him the ruling class imbibed only at feasts and banquets, and rather to acquit themselves of a social duty than from inclination. There was more drinking among the traders and merchants, but these never touched a drop until the day's business was over. The conception of the Dutch as a nation of drunkards was probably propagated by their own genre painters. But drunken scenes such as Jan Steen loved to portray were only spasmodic outbursts of a hard-working people who let themselves go on festive occasions. Those paintings depict not the normal but the exceptional.

Women, according to these foreign observers, had more to say in Holland than in other countries. In the Jacobean play *The Tragedy of Sir John van Oldenbarnevelt,* an English lady is advised by a group of Dutch women not to be a mere echo of her husband. Holland, they tell her, is a woman's paradise. There women do as they choose, they are masters, and those whom their English sisters call husbands are in Holland their servants. The men dare not even exclude them from their councils. Their influence reaches far beyond their homes. That is, no doubt, an overdrawn picture, yet truth underlies the caricature. They enforced neatness in their homes with dictatorial severity. Sir William Temple, being plagued with a cold, at a stag dinner at Burgomaster Hooft's in Amsterdam, repeatedly spat across his shoulder on the floor. He noticed that every time he did so, a servant girl brought in a mop to wipe it up. He expressed regret at causing her so much trouble, whereupon his host told him, had his wife been at home, she would have turned him out of doors for defiling her house.

Women owed their self-confidence to the good education they received. Girls were given as good elementary schooling as boys. The Calvinists insisted on that, because each child had to participate intelligently in the services of the church. The standard of elementary education, of course, was not high. Not the quality, but the extent of it, was its most striking feature. Sir Josiah Child, a contemporary of Sir William Temple, told his countrymen that "a Dutchman, however inferior in class or station he may be, always takes care that his children learn how to write a good hand and the art of counting."

Besides the common school, there was in most towns a Latin school, which was attended by sons of the professional class and the well-to-do. It had a preparatory grade where the boys were taught spelling, reading, and arithmetic. The art of writing was not taught until they had entered the Latin school proper, when they began to write and read Latin at the same time. Girls of the same social standing were not admitted there but went to the French school. The Latin schools were staffed with masters who earnestly tried to follow in the footsteps of Erasmus, and each town was ambitious for its Latin school to excel those of other cities.

A similar rivalry between the provinces kept the Dutch universities up to standard. For provincial pride would not leave Holland in sole possession of a school of higher learning. Each of the others possessed one of its own in the seventeenth century. Still, the Leyden school maintained its pre-eminence throughout the history of the Republic. Since Latin was the vehicle of instruction, the language was no bar to the attendance by foreigners. Students from all lands flocked to their classes, especially to Leyden, whose medical school was famous throughout Europe when the great Hermannus Boerhaave (1668–1738) lectured there. Theology and the ancient classics were, of course, the chief subjects of the university curriculum. But Leyden also maintained a chair for Semitic languages. Erpenius taught Arabic there, his successor Gobius compiled an Arabic grammar, and Albert Schultens became the founder of the comparative study of Semitic languages.

The greatest scholars of that age, however, were not associated with any university. Simon Stevin (d. 1620), a pioneer in the sciences of statics and hydrostatics, but versed in many other fields of research—mathematics, financial management, musical theory, civics, fortification—did lecture at Leyden for a time; but that academic connection was but a minor incident in his varied career. Hugo Grotius, escaped by a ruse from his prison in 1621, fled to Paris and became Sweden's ambassador at the court of King Louis XIII. Christian Huygens, the physicist, who solved the mystery of the motion of light, was, like Grotius, of patrician birth and considered a professor's chair no seat of honor and a professor's salary no bait. Anton van Leeuwenhoek, who discovered the existence of a microbial fauna, was a humble burgher untrained in the knowledge of Latin which alone could have admitted him to a chair in the university. Jacob Swammerdam, who proved the fundamental oneness of animal and insect life, was financially independent, and too jealous of his freedom to covet a professorship. And Spinoza, being a Jew, was not eligible to academic office. For Dutch tolerance did not go the length of disregarding creed in the appraisal of learning. A scholar who did not belong to the Dutch Reformed Church could not be entrusted with the instruction of youth.

Still, none of these men was an amateur. They were experts in every detail of their science, down to the manufacture of the tools they employed. They were akin to the great navigators and explorers of that age with whom they shared an insatiable thirst for knowledge. The seafaring men had no conception of the research that went into the composition of Stevin's handbook on the method of determining position at sea. But the urge that was behind the scholar's effort and the lust for discovery that the navigator, thanks to Stevin's guidance, could indulge to his heart's content, were fundamentally the same. The will to know impelled them both; they only differed in the aim and the method of their search.

The map of the world still bears witness to the inquisitive Dutchman's ubiquity in that age of exploration. They left it studded with Dutch names, from Spitsbergen in the arctic north down to Cape Horn at the southern extremity of the Western Hemisphere, from Staten Island and Rhode Island—names intelligible only to a Dutchman—to Tasmania and Van Diemen's Land. Abel Tasman was the Dutch skipper who circumnavigated Australia and thereby proved it to be an island. "This journey," says the English historian G. N. Clark, "added more to the knowledge of the earth's geography than any since the first journey round the world." It brought the Dutch no material profits. That continent was too distant and unproductive to make it worthwhile for Holland's merchants to trade with it. The East Indies were less far away, yet even their remoteness makes one wonder how it was possible for so small a nation to lay the foundations of a colonial empire there. In 1641 they conquered Malacca. In 1667 they took Macassar, on the south coast of Celebes, in 1677 the Sultan of Mataram, in central Java, recognized Dutch overlordship, and shortly afterward Ternate in the Moluccas was subdued. The Hollanders in their far-flung colonies in east and west did not vary their mode of life to suit the different climate. They carried with them across the seas their architecture, their domestic arts, their costumes, their manner of living. Life in Batavia must have been very much the same as life in New Amsterdam. Batavia was the richer of the two. "A noble city," it was called by Woodes Rogers, an English skipper who visited Java in 1710. That would have been sarcastic praise for Stuyvesant's New Amsterdam. But in its humble way it was a counterpart of Batavia, both being Dutch trading posts under the protection of a fort where an autocratic governor, on behalf of the company, exercised authority over a cosmopolitan and often unruly community. The Jesuit missionary, Father Jogues, who visited Manhattan in 1644, reported that there were eighteen nationalities among its population. Although Stuyvesant, a minister's son, was intolerant of other creeds than his own Reformed religion, he suffered Lutherans and Quakers and Jews to settle in New Netherland under orders of the company that was his master. The cause he served was infinitely greater than himself, and the city that grew from his New Amsterdam has inherited its tolerance from that spirit of moderation that informed the colonizing effort of the Dutch.

It was fortunate, indeed, that the ministers of the Dutch Reformed Church never became dominant in the home land. They were a domineering body of men, and often tried to dictate to the secular authorities; but the native love of independence offered them stubborn and successful resistance. If they could have had their way, the art of the theater would not have flourished at Amsterdam. Music was equally suspect with the guardians of public morals. They would have the organ played in church only for the accompaniment of the psalm singing; the evening organ recitals, which were given in many cities by order of the burgomasters, took place over their protests. The magistrates were, as a rule, on the side of liberalism and progress. The Reverend Balthazar Bekker, unique among his kind for his refusal to accept church-approved beliefs without examination, published in 1691 *Betoverde Wereld* (The World Bewitched), of which in 1700 an English translation appeared under the title *The World Turn'd Upside Down*. It was a well-conducted argument against the belief in devils, magic, and witchcraft. The Synod of North Holland unfrocked him, but the Amsterdam government continued to pay him his full minister's salary until his death in 1698.

Among a people so stubbornly attached to their individual opinions and freedom of action, there were many earnest souls who found the dogmatic discipline imposed by the church an irksome and intolerable tyranny. It is not unlikely that the most truly religious were found, in those days, outside the church. They were the mystically inclined, who prized their own religious experience above creeds and confessions. But even these individualists felt the need of a communal bond. Small groups of pietists met for the purpose of discussion and reading. The best known among these was the College so called, which started as a meeting of Arminians at Rijnsburg, near Leyden. These had been deprived of their minister through the verdict of the Synod of Dordrecht which forbade all followers of Arminius the pulpit. The Rijnsburg Collegiants, as they were called, met with an understanding response from the Mennonites who felt attracted toward their undogmatic pietism. But also among the liberal-minded oligarchy there were many who joined the Rijnsburg College. It was there, also, that Spinoza found congenial company after the Synagogue of Amsterdam had excommunicated him.

Religious movements from abroad added to the diversity of devotional thought and practice. Jean de Labadie enjoyed a temporary vogue among high society and persuaded, among other distinguished proselytes, Anna Maria van Schuurman, famous for her learning and her wit, to forsake the study of books and join his communal flock. Jacob Boehme had many followers, to judge from the fact that all his writings were available in Dutch translations. The Quakers, too, drew many Protestants away from the Reformed Church. William Caton was in charge of their mission work in the early sixties. He found a zealous helper in Judith Sewel, the first Dutch woman preacher among the Friends. It was her son, Willem Sewel, who wrote the first authoritative history of the sect, a book that, a century after its appearance, aroused the admiration of Charles Lamb, who called it "worth all ecclesiastical history put together."

The Catholics also made converts, in spite of the watchful hostility of the Calvinists. The Dutch Reformed Church proclaimed in its confession of faith that "the office of the magistracy is to prevent and to eradicate all idolatry and false religion and to destroy the kingdom of the Anti-Christ." But the States never acted according to that ecclesiastical doctrine. They refused to see a crime in adherence to Rome. Many families had retained their devotion to the Mother Church all through the Eighty Years' War. As Hollanders they could approve the revolt against a foreign ruler estranged from his subjects; as faithful Catholics they denied that the breach with His Catholic Majesty involved a breach with His Holiness the Pope. Theirs was, indeed, a conditional loyalty, for ecclesiastical doctrine allowed them to submit to a heretical government only as long as there was no hope of successful resistance. But the rulers of the Republic did not take that theory too seriously. They left quiet Catholic citizens unmolested, connived at their meetings for purposes of worship, but, to humor the Calvinists, excluded them from all public offices.

The most famous among these Roman converts was Holland's leading poet, Joost van den Vondel. The artist and mystic in him remained unmoved and unsatisfied by the bare simplicity of the Mennonite worship in which he was brought up. Catholic ritual appealed to his emotional nature. His irenic disposition caused him to be distressed at the spectacle of Calvinism excommunicating the Arminians for their rejection of the doctrine of predestination, of theological controversy injecting its venom into the body politic, till it was racked by convulsions of civil war and judicial murder. He yearned for a universal religion in which all denominations should be merged. But such conformity demanded concessions that no sect was willing to make, and Vondel made his peace with Rome as the one church that came nearest to his ideal.

Vondel the poet did not belong, with the scientists and navigators, among the explorers and discoverers of that age. He had a magnificent mastery of language, but he used it for themes that he borrowed from others. In the heyday of his genius he was satisfied to follow in the footsteps of the Greek and Latin masters whom he knew to be greater than himself. Much of the beauty of his verse is marred for the modern reader by his tendency to see the life around him as a modern counterpart of ancient Rome. He wrote not for the masses. Their poet was Jakob Cats, a didactic moralist, who expressed his homely wisdom in easily understood language. Vondel's poetry is akin to the baroque art of Rubens, the verse of Cats belongs to the type of home that one sees in the paintings of De Hooch and Vermeer. Which is tantamount to saying that, of the two, Cats gave a truer—that is, a more thoroughly Dutch—expression of the spirit of his people and his age. He was the most widely read author of his day. His collected works and the Bible were the two books that every Dutch household possessed and read with reverence.

Constantijn Huygens, the father of the great physicist, was a poet of distinction. He wrote a great deal of autobiographic verse that mirrors the life of his time. But one sees it as in a glass darkly, for he affected a terse and artificial diction that often obscured the meaning. In the choice of his subject matter he was not very different from Cats, in style he was his very opposite, one prolix, the other concise.

The historian Hooft, to whom I have referred before, was also a poet of exquisite lyrics. He too found his models, as did Vondel, in Roman antiquity and in contemporary Italy. The one poet who was both a great artist and a discoverer of new beauty was Gerbrand Adriaenszoon Bredero. He died young, but his collected works, containing comedies, farces, and lyrical poetry, reveal him as the most original and gifted fellow artist of the great genre painters of the Dutch school.

In those days, the painter was not so much an artist in our modern sense as an artisan. He had to belong to his local guild, and worked, like any craftsman, with assistants and apprentices. Painting was, consequently, not a pursuit taken up by Dutch patricians. The majority of the Dutch masters came from the middle class. Rembrandt was the son of a Leyden miller, Frans Hals of a Haarlem linen weaver, De Hooch of a Rotterdam mason, and many were of humbler birth. But the just appraisal of posterity has exalted them above their social betters. The proud patricians who had their portraits done by Hals and Rembrandt are now mostly forgotten nonentities. They sat for them in their Sunday best with all their finery to proclaim their opulence. Three centuries after their deaths they are worth even more, in effigy, than they ever were alive. From investors of wealth they have become investments, thanks to the magic of the miller's and the linen weaver's sons who, godlike, re-created them in more enduring mold than mortal flesh.

An age-old technical tradition alone cannot account for the excellence of the works of the Dutch school. Other contributory factors came into play. These painters were such consummate craftsmen because they acquired their skill at an age at which the mind is most malleable and receptive. A boy whose fingers itched to ply the brush was apprenticed to a local master at the age of ten. By that time he knew the three R's, and that knowledge was all he needed from school. Life would complete his general education. This gave the artist in him an early start. He learned to draw by methods that our age has taught us to despise. He was given drawings of the master to copy, and had to draw from casts, before he was set to copy life itself. Progress was rapid, for practice was continuous. The apprentice rose with the sun and retired with the sun and had to work all day.

The work turned out by the apprentices belonged to the master. It was the product of his workshop and he could sell it for his own. There was nothing reprehensible in that. When we order a chair from a cabinetmaker we do not inquire whether our purchase is the work of the master or of one of his assistants. If the master is willing to sell it, he vouches for its quality. In the same way the artist, in selling a painting by one of his pupils, vouched for its excellence. A burgher who wanted to buy a picture went to the workshop that turned out the kind he liked. But he was not inquisitive as to which hand of the many at work there had painted the canvas or panel of his choice.

Another cause of excellence in the average was the tendency of these painters to strive for perfection within a limited range. Nearly all of them were specialists in one narrowly circumscribed genre. The genius of Rembrandt could not be restrained within such limited bounds. But he was a rare exception. Most members of the craft achieved mastery by self-restriction. In this way each genre was split up in subsidiary genres, each of which had its specialists. The still-life artists can be subdivided into painters of breakfast tables, of fowl, of fish, of venison, of fruit, of flowers; the landscape artists in painters of winter scenes, of river and city views, of woodland, of mountain scenery.

Landscape painted for its own sake and not as background to a portrait or a scene of human activity was essentially a Dutch invention. Carel van Mander, who fled from Flanders to Holland in the early seventeenth century, wrote in verse a handbook of the art of painting for the instruction of young Dutch artists. He belonged to those who introduced the Italian manner into the Netherlands, and taught a wholly mechanical composition of the landscape. He thought of landscape painting as a form of storytelling, or more exactly perhaps, as an illustration of literature. But though Van Mander had a great name among Dutch artists as the biographer of the Dutch masters of the fifteenth and sixteenth centuries, his didacticism could not persuade the painters of Holland to adopt the stage composition of the Italians.

They painted their land as they saw it, not according to rules taught in books. Holland's land- and seascape painters were pioneers in that they gave to Europe a new vision of natural scenery. It took a long time before their leadership was acknowledged and accepted. Even a hundred years later, the great Lessing, in his *Laokoon,* still conceived of landscape painting in Van Mander's style as an art of illustration that had to visualize the imaginative scenery of the poets. As if painters were not poets in their own right!

These men lived in an age of almost continuous warfare. Yet their art is neither a satire on war nor a glorification of war. They ignored war with the supreme contempt of creative spirits for the fury of destruction. The peace of the sunlit home was the theme Vermeer and De Hooch loved best. Ruysdael sought solitude in the woods and dunes around Haarlem. If Rembrandt painted scenes of war, it was of man at war with his inmost self. And Hals, who lived nearest to the most perilous period of the Eighty Years' conflict with Spain, was the painter of laughter and the joy of living.

They did not care for heroics. They painted the simple scene of their workaday burgher world, the parlor, the kitchen, the schoolroom, the workshop, the church, the market place, the farmstead, the harbor, the beach, the sea. They were explorers akin to the navigators and the scientists of that inquisitive age, and discovered beauty where no one had suspected it—at their own door. Its omnipresence brought to light by them was a revelation no less startling than Leeuwenhoek's disclosure of the microbe's ubiquity. In that discovery lies the great, enduring merit of the Dutch school.

CHAPTER IX

The Periwig Period

THE EIGHTEENTH century is not a glorious period of Dutch history. The wars with France had taxed the economic and spiritual strength of the nation to the breaking point, and the effects of the strain became apparent in the years of peace that followed the signing of the Treaty of Utrecht. Life flowed on through its accustomed channels, but no longer with the driving force that nerved all activities in the preceding century. Its course became sluggish. The posterity of De Witt's and De Ruyter's contemporaries preferred ease to exertion, tranquillity to bustle, and the enjoyment of wealth to its pursuit.

The nineteenth century gave to its immediate predecessor the name of *Pruikentijd,* that is, Periwig Period. When the Dutch had ceased to wear wigs, they saw in the antiquated fashion a badge of decadence. The artificial head of powdered hair with its stiff, permanent wave seemed to them an emblem of effeminacy and all the foibles that were charged to that inactive age.

There is some truth, indeed, in this unflattering picture of the eighteenth-century Dutch. But the periwig does not deserve condemnation as an emblem of the national lethargy. It was worn all over Europe. The fashion that was in vogue among the English when Clive and Warren Hastings built a colonial empire cannot symbolize unmanliness in the contemporary Dutch. The successors of Jan de Witt adorned themselves with powdered periwigs not because they were effeminate weaklings, but because in fashions they followed the lead of France. They were weak, no doubt, in comparison to the founders and builders of the Republic. But there was no sign of degeneracy or decay. A sense of lassitude prevailed. The high wave of national life had sunk and flattened into a deep, smooth trough. The energy that had driven it to its towering height was not lost but only dormant, and would recover strength, in this needed period of rest, for a new upsurge of the nation's vitality. That upsurge was, indeed, slow in coming. It would take the people more than a hundred years to recover its *élan,* but all through that century the signs of the coming awakening were in evidence. The Periwig Period, with all its faults and foibles, retained a residue of strength that saved it from loss of self-respect and dignity.

Outwardly the country still presented a picture of prosperity and well-being. Foreign travelers repeated the praises of earlier visitors. The neat houses, the clean streets, the absence of beggars, the many houses of charity, were commended as admirable contrasts to conditions abroad. Scholars and learned dilettantes came from all parts of Europe to inspect the many private collections. The proud owner of such a treasure house or cabinet, as it was called, was always glad to show his paintings or books or curios to connoisseurs who came to him with reliable credentials.

Love of art and interest in science were the redeeming traits of this self-satisfied age. Conspicuous waste was everywhere in evidence. The rich vied with each other in the building of sumptuous summer homes, but though there was vulgarity in the eagerness to display their wealth, that display itself was in good taste. There were many among them who dabbled in science and philosophy, and a few rose above the dilettante level. Others patronized literature and the stage. But neither produced much in that age that had more than ephemeral value. Dutch drama was a soulless reproduction of French models, and the upper classes, taking their cue from the stadtholder's court at The Hague, preferred the French to the native theater.

To speak French, to follow French fashions, and ape French manners was the vogue among high society. The fear and distrust of France as a political power never impaired the prestige of Paris as the home of culture and good literature. Children of good families were taught to correspond in French before they could compose a letter in Dutch, and there were men in high office who never learned to write their native language with clarity and ease.

However, the best literature the century produced in Holland was written under English influence. Justus van Effen, the editor of *De Nederlandsche Spectator,* followed the lead of Addison and Steele. But it is characteristic of the Frenchness of this age that he made his literary début with an imitation of his English model in the French language. His knowledge of English literature and his mastery of French made him a literary mediator between the two countries. He translated, among other works, De Foe's *Robinson Crusoe* into French and spread knowledge on the Continent about other English books and authors by reviews in French periodicals. Later in the century, Elizabeth Wolff and Agatha Deken, working in partnership, wrote successful novels in Richardson's epistolary manner. Though much verse was written, little poetry was produced. The eighteenth century was, from the literary point of view, a barren period.

Nor did it yield any better harvest in the field of art. The painter Gerard de Lairesse dictated to his three sons, in his blind old age, a theory of painting in which he taught that "Nature is *modern,* that is to say imperfect, but again she is *antique* and perfect when one knows how to fit out the landscape with strange and beautiful buildings, tombs, and such like remains of ancient Rome which constitute an *antique* landscape."

This Dutch precursor of Lessing, though he belonged to

the late seventeenth century, was in taste and mannerism a true representative of the Periwig Period. That age dressed nature up in what it called the Greek or Roman style. It sought perfect beauty in the unnatural. Its art suffered from that striving for perfection through adornment. The gardens of the rich, the landscapes that they had painted, the poetry they admired were travesties of nature's simple beauty.

The lassitude into which the nation lapsed was responsible for the Republic's withdrawal from active participation in the affairs of Europe. The power that in the days of Prince William III had stood in the forefront of the continental opposition against French imperialism was now content to remain in the background and feared nothing more than to be drawn into the vortex of another European war. Its foreign policy had for its aim the maintenance of the Peace of Utrecht. The alliance with England endured, but it had ceased to be a partnership of equals. The seven ships of state of the United Provinces were taken in tow by the British man-of-war.

There was friction with Austria over the Barrier Treaty, but, thanks to the persistent cleavage between the Bourbon and Hapsburg dynasties, the emperor was conciliatory, since he needed the good will of the maritime powers. For the same reason he settled the dispute over the Ostend Company to the satisfaction of Holland and England. That company was to inaugurate a colonial enterprise of the southern Netherlands, in competition with the Dutch and English East India companies. But the emperor, who needed the consent of the maritime powers to the succession of his daughter, Maria Theresa, yielded to their demand that the company be dissolved rather than incur their certain enmity by persisting in an enterprise of whose success he could not be sure anyhow.

The man who was responsible for the Republic's foreign policy at this time was Simon van Slingelandt, Pensionary of

Holland. He was, indeed, no typical representative of the Periwig Period. He proved himself an able, forceful statesman, who had the knowledge correctly to diagnose the ailments from which the Union was suffering and the courage to propose a treatment for their cure.

The antiquated machinery of the Union was badly in need of renovation. The slowness with which it functioned was a laughing stock among the foreign envoys at The Hague. Van Slingelandt proposed as a remedy that the Council of State be reinvested with its former authority. He realized that such a reform would reduce the members of the Union to greater dependence on one another. But which is better, he asked in reply to that objection, "to let the State perish or to apply remedies for its salvation which somewhat circumscribe provincial freedom?" "Besides," he dared add to that question, "the rulers all too often defend their own interests under the slogan of vindicating liberty. Our ancestors, who sacrificed all they possessed for liberty, realized too well that Freedom has its limits, and that there is nothing more injurious to Freedom than Freedom itself when it oversteps those limits."

He further proposed that the deputies to the assemblies of the provincial States and States-General should be instructed in advance instead of having to travel back to their capitals for directions on how to vote. And finally he wanted authority set up for compelling delinquent provinces to carry their share of the federal burden.

His recommendations were listened to with respect; they were read in manuscript by successive generations of magistrates and functionaries; they were published in print in 1784, nearly seventy years after they were made. But nothing was done to turn his wisdom into practice. The vested interests that throve on the perpetuation of abuses were powerful enough to block all attempts at reform.

The ruling families in town and province had gradually

become closed corporations that admitted no outsiders into their fenced-off domain. They looked upon the sphere of their authority as virtually their private hunting ground. They filled by co-option any vacancies in the town councils, disposed of all offices within the grant of the government, divided them among themselves, and sold the minor jobs to relatives and protégés. They drew up regular contracts by which they bound each other to reciprocity in favors and to permanent exclusion of undesirables. There were many who, while drawing the incomes from remunerative jobs, hired others to do the work at a fraction of the salary. There were burgomasters who presented their newborn babes with such plums, and left the stones by way of favor to an indigent substitute. Such a system did not insure the rise to power of the best minds. On the contrary, men of character and courage were feared rather than favored, and kept out of office by the conspiracy of powerful mediocrity. Simon van Slingelandt became Pensionary of Holland in spite, not because of, his pre-eminence. In 1720, after Heinsius' death, the office was not offered to him, though none was better qualified to fill the vacancy. Seven years later, however, the international situation called for a man who was able to grapple with it, and reluctantly the men in power made him Pensionary, but not without exacting from him a promise that he would not re-establish the stadtholderate. And when Slingelandt died in 1736, his successor, Anthony van der Heim, was given an instruction that definitely forbade him to attempt any change in the existing form of government.

Yet it was only too clear to the thoughtful whose judgment was not blinded by self-interest that without drastic reforms there was small hope for the Union to recover from its state of collapse. A deluge of political pamphlets voiced the public's anxiety and criticism. In these the Periwig Period has supplied the historian with plenty of evidence against itself, which is, perhaps, the most convincing proof that its case was not hopeless. The complacency that was the besetting sin of the ruling class did not affect the nation as a whole.

A serious disturbance of the political equilibrium in Europe brought the forces of discontent to the fore. In 1740 the emperor, Charles VI, passed away, and the male line of the Hapsburgs became extinct. The succession of his daughter Maria Theresa seemed assured by the Pragmatic Sanction, which nearly all the powers had agreed to support. The emperor had made great sacrifices to obtain their consent. He had ceded the two Sicilies to Spain, Lorraine to France, and dissolved the Ostend Company to placate the maritime powers. But after his death the succession was claimed by Charles Albert, Elector of Bavaria, as the nearest male descendant of Ferdinand I, and when Frederick II of Prussia came to his support and invaded Silesia, the young empress appealed to the guarantors of the Pragmatic Sanction for aid. Against their will the States-General were again involved in the conflict.

They gave but halfhearted support. France, though a signatory of the Pragmatic Sanction, allied herself with Bavaria and Prussia, invaded the Austrian Netherlands, and occupied the Barrier towns. The federal army was helpless, while the provinces quarreled among themselves as to who should be chief in command. Friesland insisted that its stadtholder, Prince William IV, son and heir of John William Friso, should be appointed, and when Holland refused her assent threatened to stop all payments. The Orangists were, as always, the war party. Their opponents, who feared lest the prince, once at the head of the army, should seize political power too, wanted the Republic to remain neutral. Amsterdam and the States of Holland were in favor of a separate peace with France, and the French government, aware of this, sought to scare the Dutch war party into falling in with Holland's wishes by invading Dutch territory. But this move had the opposite effect. As soon as French troops entered Zeeland, the masses rose and demanded the reinstatement of the prince. The selfish oligarchy suddenly caved in. The provincial States elected William IV stadtholder, first Zeeland, then Holland, Utrecht, and Overijsel. The States-General, no less alarmed by the popular clamor, appointed him commander in chief of army and navy. There was no more talk of a separate peace. The prince, on the contrary, wanted closer co-operation with England. But the Republic was only a feeble ally. Fortunately for the Dutch, there was war weariness on every side. The French and English wanted peace no less eagerly than they. Maintenance of the political order of Europe as established by the Treaty of Utrecht was agreed upon by all. The peace of Aix-la-Chapelle restored the status quo ante. The Republic, accordingly, regained its Barrier towns, not through any determined action of its own, but thanks to the general desire for compromise and peace. The restitution of the Barrier was a worthless present. For the fortifications had been demolished, and the Republic lacked the money to restore them. The towns in their defenseless condition were sad reminders of the low state to which the once powerful Republic had fallen.

William IV was not the kind of man to make good use of the almost dictatorial authority thrust upon him. He was the first Prince of Orange to be elected stadtholder in all the seven provinces, and each province had made the office hereditary in both the male and female lines. Fear of a popular uprising had changed the oligarchs into fawning servants of His Highness. Unfortunately, William's feeble constitution made him disinclined to forceful action. The clamor of the masses had brought him to power, but his timorous mind was suspicious of popular movements. Being a conservative by nature, he felt a closer affinity to the class that had barred him from power than to the mass to which he owed it. And pleased by their servility he befriended the oppressors instead of the oppressed, who were his real friends.

One reform, however, brought permanent improvement, but for this the man in the street, not the prince, deserves the credit. The iniquitous system of farming out the collection of taxes had been the butt of pamphleteers and pothouse politicians for many decades. But now that the war had paralyzed various industries, unemployment and hunger embittered the working classes, and in that ugly mood they translated the sarcasms of scribblers and topers into violent action. The tax farmers, who used spies and extortionist methods to squeeze all they could get out of the taxpayers, were the best-hated men in the Republic. When the prince did not act to put an end to the abuse, the people took the matter into their own hands. In several towns of Holland the houses of the tax collectors were wrecked by angry rioters, and only the menace of worse tumults extorted from the authorities the abolition of the rotten practice.

Prince William IV died in 1751, leaving a three-year-old son, for whom his widow, Anne, daughter of King George II, acted as regent. But in 1758 Anne also died. Feeling her death approaching, she appointed Duke Lewis Ernest of Brunswick-Wolfenbüttel as guardian of the young Prince of Orange. He had been a field marshal in the imperial army, had entered the service of the States-General in that same rank, and had been appointed, in 1752, commander in chief of the federal forces. He was a skillful administrator, and succeeded by tactful maneuvering in winning the confidence of both the Orangists and the powerful opponents in Holland of the stadtholderate. Being a foreigner, he was not by tradition or prejudice committed to either faction, and could be friends with both without the surrender of any inherited loyalties. But capable though he was, the sixteen years of his residence in Holland were not conspicuous for achievement in any field of action.

When the young Prince of Orange came of age, he could, and should, have claimed the offices of stadtholder and commander in chief of army and navy, which were his by hereditary right. Instead, he humbly requested the States to confirm him in these, a proof of diffidence that marked all his actions. In 1672, young William III had unhesitatingly assumed full and absolute authority; the fifth William, on his accession, concluded with the duke a secret Act of Consultation by which he bound the German marshal to remain at court as the stadtholder's confidant and counselor. William was an erudite man, thanks to a tenacious memory that seemed unable to forget any detail of his wide and varied reading. He was a keen student of languages, history, political science, physics. But with all his knowledge he never learned how to make up his mind, though he could be stubborn about trifles. The duke planned, formulated, and disposed; the prince assented and signed on the dotted line. The duke decided that the prince should marry Wilhelmina, daughter of Augustus William, the brother of King Frederick II of Prussia, and the prince traveled to Berlin for the wedding ceremony. She was but seventeen years old, and Brunswick, who was her uncle, must have thought that through this match he had strengthened his hold upon the irresolute husband of his niece. Being a strong-willed, clever, and vivacious young woman, she resented the prince's dependence on his former guardian and did her best to arouse in him a spirit of self-assertion. But he was defenseless against a will power stronger than his own. He was capable of resistance only against the impact of new ideas on his mind. For the prince was conservative to a degree, and feared the ferment of revolutionary thought that might disturb the placid tenor of life in which he found contentment.

It was his misfortune, however, to live in an era of social unrest and political innovation. There were no great revolutionary thinkers in the Netherlands, but the Dutch were acquainted with the writings of the English rationalists, and of Montesquieu, Voltaire, Rousseau. Their ideas were widely discussed in periodicals and daily papers, of which the Republic produced a prolific crop, both in Dutch and in French. There was little opposition to the intrusion of this foreign thought. It came chiefly from ministers of the Reformed Church, the traditional guardians of the nation's spiritual heritage. But their defense of orthodoxy lacked the zeal and conviction that their seventeenth-century predecessors used to put into it. They succeeded in obtaining from the States of Holland the suppression of Rousseau's *Emile* and *Contrat Social*. That gave them at least the satisfaction of having done their duty, if not the certainty of having stemmed the evil tide. For they must have known that the effect of the ban was enhanced popularity of the forbidden books.

However, even if they could have stopped the people from reading the forbidden, it would have been of no avail. For the revolutionary message in cold print carried less persuasion than the heart-warming news that came from America. The Declaration of Independence out-argued all the clever and learned theorists of England and France. Here was a people that actually did what the others taught. The colonists did not merely talk about the sovereignty of the people, they seized it and started to govern themselves.

The dormant forces of discontent in the Republic were suddenly aroused from their lethargy. The success of bold self-assertion by others awakened in the disheartened a new courage and fresh hope. Throughout the country voices were heard acclaiming the insurgents. And these supporters of the American cause were to be found among all classes, even among the aristocracy, whose vested interests could not gain from a triumph of rebellious colonists over the mother country. One of the stanchest and most enthusiastic champions of America was Baron Joan Derk van der Capellen tot den Poll. And when the Dutch Republic had recognized the United States of America, Gijsbert Karel van Hogendorp, then a boy of just over twenty, but destined to rise to the highest political office in his country, went on a study tour through the United States, which he regarded as a laboratory where future statesmen could watch experiments in state building, government, commerce, and finance. "I wanted to know," he wrote to his mother, "how states were organized, and America is forming itself into a republic. I wanted to enlighten myself concerning finances and systems of taxation, I wanted to know the measure of power that the people can exercise, and never did people possess more of it than do the Americans. I was anxious to learn what are the surest avenues for a republic that is peacefully engaged in commerce, and it is here, where commerce is very little complicated and where a thousand attempts are being made to expand it, that I can best apply that theory and form correct ideas that will serve me as a foundation in the future."

Not all Dutch well-wishers could give such clear and considered reasons for their pro-American feelings. Many compared the struggle of their forefathers against Spain with the rising of the colonists against Great Britain. They saw the greatest episode of their own history repeated in the New World. Others again hailed the American revolt as a warning to the ruling families who allowed the Dutch people as little share in their own government as the English granted the colonists. And yet, there were members among those same families who, from sheer hatred of the House of Orange, rejoiced in the insult to the monarchy in England. From various and often opposite motives birds of different feathers flocked together. Parlor radicals who had read Rousseau, dictatorial oligarchs who hated the prince, wealthy shipowners who were hoping for an untrammeled trade with the

Americans, and disgruntled have-nots who envied the rich, formed a motley coalition of friends of the American Congress.

Unfortunately, the coalition had no staying power. There was no plan of action, no conscious organization, no common purpose. Idealism, greed, hatred, and envy did not harmonize into one leitmotiv. The policy of the States-General could not take its cue from a *vox populi* so discordant. They needed the leadership of a strong man who knew what he wanted. But the Pensionary of Holland, Pieter van Bleiswijk (1772–87), had neither strength of character nor diplomatic ability. And the prince, who had never learned to make an independent decision, lacked the courage to make up his mind where so much was at stake. His sympathies were with England. Through his mother he was related to the royal house, and his innate conservatism saw in England the defender of prerogatives that were his as well. Besides, he had inherited from his ancestors a political tradition of alliance with England and suspicion of France. He would abide by the Treaty of Alliance concluded with England in 1678.

But the interests of Dutch commerce and the honor of the flag were constantly being attacked by the English. The Dutch carried on a lucrative smuggling trade with the rebels from their Caribbean islands of St. Eustatius and Curaçao. English cruisers held up their merchantmen on the high seas and carried them off as prizes to the disgrace of the Dutch fleet, which was not strong enough to give them adequate protection. The prince, as the nominal head of the navy, had to bear the blame for its poor equipment, and was openly accused of betraying the country's interests and honor to England. The British ambassador, Sir Robert Yorke, an ill-tempered bulldog, did not use the kind of manner and language that could smooth ruffled feelings and disarm opposition. In February, 1777, he handed to the States-General a memorandum complaining that the governor of St. Eustatius,

Johannes de Graeff, had fired a salute to the flag of the rebels. Yorke demanded the recall and discharge of De Graeff and threatened that, in case of an evasive answer, His Majesty would take the proper measures due to the interests and dignity of the crown.

De Graeff was called home and examined by his masters, the directors of the West India Company. He explained that the *Andrew Doria,* the first ship to appear on the roads off St. Eustatius with the American flag in top, had saluted with eleven or thirteen shots. He had answered her with two shots less, by which the commander of the fort implied that he welcomed the *Doria* merely as a merchant vessel, regardless of the flag she flew. In other words, he had greeted the ship, not the flag, and his welcome had no political significance.

Whether this plea convinced his employers of the innocent nature of the incident is subject to doubt. But they were evidently pleased to accept it as such. The prince, who was chief director of the company, wrote to the Dutch ambassador in London that De Graeff had justified himself. "But I wish," he added, "that the defense had been communicated to the British government, and that his return to St. Eustatius had been postponed until assurance had been received that there was no objection in London to his reinstatement." The directors showed more character than His Highness. Having found their way clear to declaring the British charges baseless, they refused to ask for the accuser's permission to return him to his post.

The directors of the company were at that time, perhaps, less overawed by England's power than they had been a year before; France had recognized the young American Republic and declared war on England; and the anti-British elements in the Netherlands were wishfully predicting the approaching downfall of John Bull. Especially in Amsterdam hopes were rising high. Its rulers felt inclined to join the French-

American alliance and obtain, in return for Dutch aid, special privileges for Holland's commerce. But instead of advocating a straightforward and consistent policy in the States of Holland they resorted to backstair parleys with representatives of the American Congress. England, meanwhile, offered to ease her contraband regulations, and the States-General voted to accept her concessions allowing so-called limited convoy. They promised that masts and timber would not be carried in Dutch ships sailing under convoy, but refused to exclude all naval equipment. But a year later the British discovered timber in Dutch bottoms that were convoyed by a small squadron under Admiral van Bylandt. The guilty vessels were declared prize, and the long-standing alliance of 1678 with England was abrogated by the government in London. The States-General, thereupon, voted to revert to unlimited convoy and to equip fifty-two ships of war.

It was at this juncture, when the relations with England had become severely strained, that the Republic was invited to join the League of Armed Neutrality, under the leadership of Russia. Its aim was protection of neutral shipping on the basis of concepts that were dear to the merchants of Holland. The League declared that neutral vessels carrying enemy goods were free to trade with belligerents in noncontraband articles. The States-General joined, though Russia gave them no guarantee of armed assistance. Their adherence to the League was taken in London as a *casus belli*. The British government had just discovered evidence of Amsterdam's secret dealings with the rebels. The ship on which Henry Lawrence sailed to Holland in September, 1780, had been seized off Newfoundland, and among his papers the English captors discovered a trade agreement that the Amsterdam rulers had concluded in 1778 with an American representative at Aix-la-Chapelle. When the States-General, instead of heeding the protests from London, added insult to injury by joining the League, the British government declared war.

The opponents of the stadtholder, that strange coalition of heterogeneous elements, hailed the outbreak of war as a victory for them over the Orange party. They claimed to be the sole defenders of Dutch honor and dignity, and assumed the self-righteous name of Patriots.

The break with England, whatever sense of triumph it brought to the Patriots at home, did not raise the Republic's prestige abroad. In 1781 the States-General meekly yielded to a demand from Emperor Joseph II for the withdrawal of their garrisons from the Barrier towns. Unsupported by Great Britain, they dared not refuse. The federal fleet remained inactive. Admiral Zoutman, it is true, had an encounter, in the summer of 1780, with the British under Hyde Parker. It ended in a draw, and in the general relief that he was not beaten this negative success was hailed as a victory. But as a result of this "victory" the disabled Dutch fleet remained in hiding throughout the war, while the British swept Holland's merchant marine off the ocean.

Yet in one respect the Republic's international prestige remained unshaken. Amsterdam was still the money market of all Europe. As the chief creditors of every monarchy in Christendom the Dutch still commanded respect from an insolvent world. When the States-General resolved, without a dissenting vote, to admit and acknowledge John Adams as Envoy of the United States of America, he wrote home, with undisguised satisfaction: "The American cause has gained a signal triumph in this country"; and he quoted—at the risk, he said, of being charged with vanity—the words in which the Spanish minister at The Hague had complimented him on his achievement: "Sir, you have struck the greatest blow of all Europe. It is the greatest blow that has been struck in the American cause, and the most decisive." Shortly afterward he arranged with three Dutch banks the floating of a loan of five million guilders.

The Dutch Republic was the second country to give official recognition to the young Republic. France had taken the lead. But France had been prompted by her traditional enmity toward England. In persuading the United Provinces to follow that lead, Adams claimed "to have torn from England's bosom an intimate affectionate friend and a faithful ally of a hundred years' continuance." And he accomplished this diplomatic triumph, he said, "by availing himself only of the still small voice of reason, urging general motives and national interests, without money, without intrigue, without imposing pomp, or more imposing fame."

He should have added, "but not without the aid of the Dutch people." John Paul Jones, who despite British protests was given shelter in Holland for three months and feted as a hero wherever he went, had ample opportunity to gauge the popular mood. "The Dutch people are for us and for the war," he wrote to Bancroft in December, 1779. But four years of war made them wiser. In 1784, when peace was concluded at Paris, there was a general sense of relief. Enough had been lost to make any peace preferable to a prolongation of the conflict. International prestige, the carrying trade, and territory in India were the Republic's worst casualties.

The Patriots had small reason to pride themselves on having forced the country into war. They shifted the burden of guilt for its disastrous outcome onto the shoulders of the prince, whom they blamed for the desolate condition of the army and navy. His trusted counselor, the Duke of Brunswick, withdrew from The Hague under pressure of a vicious campaign against him, and left the country for good in 1784. The Patriots continued to agitate against the prince after the war. If they had made propaganda for the democratic ideas that had triumphed in America, they would have done a signal service to their country. Joan Derk van der Capellen did publish, anonymously, an eloquent pamphlet addressed *To the People* (1781) in which he called upon the citizens to recover their ancient rights, which he charged that the House of Orange and the provincial States assemblies had usurped; and at meetings of Patriot members of the ruling families, of noblemen in Friesland and Gelderland, of students in Utrecht, ideas were voiced that echoed those of the American colonists. But when it came to turning theory into practice, the measures proposed aimed chiefly at curtailment of the stadtholder's prerogatives. The Patriots lacked organization and skill to proceed from destructive opposition to constructive reform.

The prince, instead of protesting the illegality of the measures that whittled down his power, left The Hague and made a tour of the country, hoping that the acclaim of the rank and file, who were traditionally loyal to the House of Orange, would impress and confound the Patriots. The latter had everywhere organized volunteer corps, and in several places serious clashes occurred between these and the Orangist populace. The situation was especially tense in the city of Utrecht, where the democratic movement was better organized and conducted with more aggressiveness than elsewhere. The Orangists now began to form their own volunteer guards and to campaign for organized resistance against the encroachments of the Patriots. The prince himself did not take any active part in this countermovement. He settled down in his country seat, Het Loo, and issued a lengthy manifesto in which he defended his rights and rejected all reforms.

But the Orangists could not hope to defeat the opposition while their leader was sulking in his tent. They wanted him to reappear at The Hague and resume command of its garrison, which had been taken from him. But the prince refused, unless he were called back by the States-General or the anti-

Patriot minority of the States of Holland. But neither had the courage to defy the Patriots.

At this point the high-spirited young wife of the prince took matters into her own hands. With William's consent she traveled to Holland in hope of obtaining from one of the two pusillanimous assemblies the invitation that her husband required. But at the boundary between Holland and Utrecht she was refused admission into the province by a volunteer corps of Patriots, whose action was subsequently approved by the States of Holland.

Princess Wilhelmina wrote an indignant report of the incident to her brother King Frederick William II of Prussia. Through his ambassador at The Hague he demanded satisfaction for the insult offered his sister, and the British ambassador, Sir James Harris, also protested on behalf of his government. When the States of Holland refused to accede to these demands, the King of Prussia sent an army of twenty thousand men to the Republic. Patriot resistance collapsed immediately, the prince returned to The Hague, the Orangists everywhere came back into power, the volunteer corps was disbanded, the princess was given satisfaction by the States of Holland, which promised to punish all who were responsible for her detention, thousands of Patriots fled to safety in America and France, King Frederick's troops left the country laden with loot, and Holland paid an indemnity of half a million guilders to Prussia. The House of Orange was reinstated at the cost of its prestige. It was a tottering rule that could be stabilized only with the aid of foreign intervention.

Its unsteadiness became apparent at the first flare-up of democratic aspirations beyond the border. The storm that rose in France soon swept northward across the Netherlands. French revolutionary troops under Dumouriez overran the Austrian Netherlands, and the French Convention declared them annexed. Dutch Patriots who had fled to France in

1788 had formed a Batavian legion under Colonel Daendels and hoped to return to their native land as fellows-in-arms of Dumouriez's soldiers. But Dumouriez suffered a setback and betrayed the cause of the Revolution. The combined forces of England, Austria and the Republic seemed able to safeguard the United Provinces against invasion. Then, however, new forces came surging up from the French volcano, and poured their lava over the Low Countries. The English withdrew their troops, and the army of Pichegru, finding no formidable obstacle left in its way, crossed the frozen rivers into Holland. No resistance was attempted; on the contrary, the bringers of fraternity, equality, and liberty were hailed by the Patriots as brothers and friends. On January 19, 1795 Colonel Daendels entered Amsterdam unopposed, at the head of his Batavian legion. The day before Prince William had written a letter of farewell to the States-General and the States of Holland, and sailed at midnight in a fishing smack for England.

The name Batavian borne by the Dutch legion under Daendels had political significance. The Patriots could not distinguish between the forces of reaction personified in William V and the republican government of earlier days. In their romantic excitement they damned alike the Union of Utrecht and the structure it had supported for two centuries. The exiled stadtholder had been a weaker, but not a more wicked, tyrant than his predecessors. But their wickedness was not a personal fault, it was rooted in the system they represented. They were usurpers of the people's liberties because the Union of Utrecht had willed it so. To recover those liberties the people had to revert to the pristine days of the Batavi, one of those Germanic tribes known to Tacitus, who gave a dramatic account of its revolt against the Romans. The ancient freedom of the Batavi was to be restored to their posterity under a new dispensation, the Batavian Republic.

CHAPTER X

The Monarchy

THE REVOLUTION that swept away the Dutch Republic of the Seven United Netherlands and established the Batavian Republic in its stead was accomplished without bloodshed. Everywhere the representatives of the old regime yielded meekly to the restorers of Batavian freedom. But the millennium that the Patriots had predicted did not materialize. Freedom, they soon learned, could not be won with foreign aid. The French savior was not a disinterested benefactor. He wanted payment for the labor of liberation, he demanded Dutch support in defending and spreading the revolution. The Batavian Republic had to pay a hundred million guilders for its liberty, had to quarter, feed, and clothe twenty-five thousand French soldiers, be responsible for their pay, and conclude with republican France an offensive and defensive alliance. That meant involvement in her war with England, blockade of the Dutch coast by the British navy, paralysis of Holland's merchant marine, loss of colonies in the East and West Indies, unemployment at home, and widespread poverty among the working class.

The sovereign Batavian people discovered also, to their dismay, that the building of a political home for their new freedom was a work of art that baffled the inexperience of the architects. They quarreled among themselves over the blueprints. Some wanted to remodel the federal system of the Dutch Republic. Others proposed to build an entirely new structure that would replace the separate homes of the Seven

United Provinces. And there were, of course, the mediators who believed that there was a middle ground where federalists and unitarists, as the extremists were called, could meet.

Little of enduring value was accomplished by the Batavian Republic. The instability of its government frustrated the best intentions of the reformers. The States-General made way for a National Assembly, this again, in 1798, for a Constituent Assembly, then, three years later, came fresh changes intended to appease the moderates by a partial return to federalism. Constant interference, first by the Paris Directory, then by Napoleon, in the internal affairs of the Republic and passive resistance by the Orangist majority of the nation increased the difficulties of the Batavian rulers. The ablest among these was Rutger Jan Schimmelpenninck. He seems to have been the only one in whom Napoleon, emperor since 1804, had any confidence. The latter suspected the Batavian government of secret hostility to France, and determined to replace it by a one-man rule. The Legislative Body, reduced from thirty-five to nineteen members, was to remain, but the executive power would be vested in a Pensionary, who would be assisted by a Council of State of five members, by five Secretaries of State, and a Secretary General.

The constitution embodying these reforms was drafted by Schimmelpenninck, who at the time was Batavian envoy at Paris. He was designated for the office of Pensionary, and entered upon his function on April 29, 1805. In the one year of his administration more was accomplished than in the decade preceding it. It had an efficient taxation system and a Primary Education Act to its credit. But Schimmelpenninck was not given time for further improvements and consolidation of his rule. In 1806 the emperor, possessed with the ambition to extend the power of the Bonaparte dynasty, decided to make his brother Louis King of Holland. The Patriots had no choice. They were ordered to accept the new form of government. If they refused, he warned them, the

Republic would be annexed. The Council of State, the Legislature, and the Secretaries, assembled in joint session, decided to yield, and signed the treaty with France under which Napoleon guaranteed the new kingdom's independence. Schimmelpenninck refused to ratify it, resigned his office, and transferred his authority to the president of the legislative body. A deputation from the Republican government was received in audience by Napoleon and humbly requested him to appoint his brother Louis King of Holland.

Louis Bonaparte tried his very best to turn himself into a Dutchman. He had a gentle disposition and actually won the affection of his subjects. Orangists emerged from sulking self-effacement under the Batavian Republic, and offered him their services. Willem Bilderdijk, gloomy dean of Dutch letters, who had gone into voluntary exile in 1796, returned to Holland, accepted an appointment as the king's librarian, and taught his royal master Dutch. As a romantic believer in feudalism and in royalty by the grace of God he could reconcile himself with the new regime, though it owed its rise to imperial, rather than divine, grace. Even luminaries of Batavian liberty were not averse to service under the monarchy. Most of Schimmelpenninck's secretaries of state remained in office, and the former commander of the Batavian legion, H. W. Daendels, became governor general of the Dutch East Indies.

The constitution proclaimed by the king on August 7, 1806, was little different from the one it superseded. The introduction of the monarchy was its chief innovation. New also was the official use of the name Holland for the entire kingdom. Wherever it occurred, in the foregoing story, it stood for the dominant province among the Seven United Netherlands. Its application to the full extent of their united territory gave official sanction to a usage long established by the speech of both natives and foreigners.

Royal power had never been popular among the Dutch.

The tyranny of Philip II had bred in them a hatred of kingship. There were critical moments, as we saw, in the history of the Republic when the stadtholder then in power could have made himself monarch. But awareness, no doubt, of that latent aversion to a one-man rule withheld each of them from taking the decisive step. It was, indeed, a blessing in disguise that the monarchy was forced upon the nation by Napoleon. The ancient factions of Orangists and Patriots could never have joined in proclaiming the seven provinces a united kingdom. Louis Bonaparte made the monarchy of the Oranges possible. When the Prince of Orange came back from exile in 1813, he returned among people who, under foreign rule, had been unified into a nation.

It was a hard, despotic school in which the Dutch learned and practiced unity. Not King Louis was the despot. His imperial brother accused him of courting popularity, of being too easy with his subjects, of failing to enforce the law against trade with England and conniving at the lucrative smuggling trade. In 1809, the English landed in Zeeland, and although the expedition finally miscarried, it had brought proof that the emperor's continental fortress was not invulnerable. Napoleon welcomed the incident as a pretext for his brother's removal. King Louis was summoned to Paris and forced to sign a treaty by which he ceded all the land south of the Maas, promised strict prohibition of all commerce with England, accepted customs inspection by imperial appointees, and submitted to occupation of the river mouths by an army corps of eighteen thousand men. But when Oudinot, the commander of these troops, received orders from Napoleon to occupy Amsterdam, which Louis had made his capital, the latter resigned on behalf of his second son. But by that time his brother had decided upon incorporation of the kingdom with the empire. A proclamation to that effect appeared in the *Moniteur* of July 10, 1810.

For three years the Dutch nation possessed no political

entity. Their country had become part of the Napoleonic Empire, and French officials directed its administration. Among them were men of refinement and culture. Charles François Lebrun, the governor general, was a man of letters by avocation. General Molitor, who commanded the Seventeenth Division with headquarters at Amsterdam, was a humane officer and was generally liked by the Dutch. The prefect De Celles was unpopular, but the people could not help respecting him for the skill and honesty with which he conducted his administration. These men ruled a recalcitrant and unwilling populace with tact and forbearance and acquitted themselves in irreproachable manner of a task that probably was distasteful to them.

Holland owes a debt of gratitude to that Napoleonic administration. The Dutch, though they prayed for deliverance from bondage, proved that they appreciated its blessings by preserving the governmental machinery when they had recovered their independence. There was little in the system inherited from their national past that could compare with it in efficiency. Even the most reactionary eulogists of the good old days had to confess that the smoothly running machinery imported from Paris was a vast improvement on the Dutch Republic's complicated mechanism that was chronically out of order. When the Prince of Orange returned to his own in 1813, he could do no better than take the French system over —lock, stock, and barrel. Justice was promptly administered without favoritism or graft, taxes were more evenly imposed and were less of a burden than before, the police system was severe but impartial, the military system a model of organization. The provinces, now called departments, and the municipalities had never before been governed with such efficiency and orderliness. The Dutch people's first reaction was to hate these alien innovations; then they became reconciled to them; and finally, when they were free to discard every one of them, they gratefully adopted them.

This is the more remarkable as the three years of French rule left bitter memories behind. Holland was drained of her wealth. The strict enforcement of Napoleon's continental system, which was to bring England to her knees, paralyzed Dutch commerce. In order to reduce the national debt, the emperor ordered the reduction of the interest on the debt to one-third, a measure that worked hardships on the many whose scant incomes came from investments in state funds. But nothing created more resentment than the introduction of military conscription, which forced the youth of the country to enlist in Napoleon's armies. Fifteen thousand Dutch boys marched with the emperor into Russia, and only a few hundred returned to tell the story of their sufferings.

In the early days of November, 1813, rumors reached Holland of Napoleon's defeat at Leipzig. On November 14, the French garrison withdrew from Amsterdam to Utrecht by order of Lebrun. That was the signal for a popular uprising on the following day, which has gone down in history by the name of *Bijltjesdag*, that is, Hatchet Day. But no hatchets were swung at the heads of hated Frenchmen. The men who started the riots were themselves called *Bijltjes*. They were the carpenters employed in the shipyards along the water front of Amsterdam. By a common transfer of meaning they were known by the name that properly belonged to the tool of their trade. They were a rowdy and unruly lot but ardent patriots and supporters of the House of Orange. They proceeded, on the evening of November 15, to set fire to the customhouses, hated symbols of French rapacity. But they were a good-natured crowd out for fun rather than vengeance. Still, this sudden outburst scared the French authorities out of their wits. Lebrun fled to Utrecht the next day and De Celles followed in his track, although the National Guard had little difficulty in restoring order.

At The Hague, meanwhile, Dutch freedom was proclaimed in less riotous fashion. The leadership there was in the hands of aristocrats, foremost among whom was Gijsbert Karel van Hogendorp, who, in his early twenties, had visited the young American Republic. With him were associated the Count van Limburg-Stirum, and Van der Duyn van Maasdam. When news of the *Bijltjesdag* outbreak reached The Hague, Van Limburg-Stirum, wearing Orange colors, marched at the head of the National Guard to the City Hall, where he read a proclamation drawn up by Van Hogendorp. The triumvirate, not meeting with the hoped-for response from their social equals, but assured that the middle class was in a ferment, constituted themselves, November 21, a provisional government, and sent two envoys to London to invite the Prince of Orange to return to The Hague.

The significance of Van Hogendorp's action was in its anticipation of any outside attempt to liberate Holland. He wanted the nation's freedom to be its own achievement, not a present from Great Britain and her allies. Bands of Cossacks, it is true, and a Prussian corps under Von Bülow entered the country soon afterward and helped to clinch the work of deliverance. But by that time the self-appointed government was in the saddle and had released all Hollanders from their sworn obedience to Napoleon.

On November 30, the Prince of Orange landed on the beach of Scheveningen. He was the son of the exiled stadtholder, William V, who had died at Brunswick in 1806. A proclamation, issued at Amsterdam on December 2, declared: "It is not William the Sixth whom the Dutch nation has called back. It is William the First who as Sovereign Prince appears among the people."

Sovereign prince was to be his title. He had declined the name of king, not from any fear of ancient prejudices, but in the hope of assuming the crown at a more auspicious occasion. For he knew that he was destined to rule over a greatly enlarged kingdom that was to include the Austrian Netherlands. It was England that, for her own security, insisted on this expansion of his realm. She wanted a strong and self-reliant state on the Continent opposite England that would counterbalance French ambitions, the old device of the Barrier fortresses revived on a much larger scale. King William I was to be England's sentry on the northern frontier of France.

The consent of the Emperor of Austria was needed for this scheme, as he had to be indemnified for the loss of his Dutch provinces. His allies, England, Prussia, and Russia, presented him with extensive territory in North Italy as a substitute. The inhabitants whose lands were involved in this barter were not consulted. Those of the Austrian Netherlands were simply told by the four great powers that they thus disposed of their country "in virtue of their right of conquest."

To soothe their wounded feelings the proposed "enlargement" of Holland was christened a "union" of the two. It was a reunion of the twins that had gone their separate ways in the late sixteenth century. They did not meet with transports of joy. The south was solidly Catholic, and the Roman clergy objected to a monarch whom the Netherlands constitution required to be of the Protestant religion. To the inhabitants their inclusion in the kingdom of the Netherlands was a resubmission to foreign rule rather than a partnership with their nearest relations. There was, it is true, a similarity of speech between Flemings and Dutch, but that linguistic bond was weakened by the religious cleavage. The southerners outnumbered the Dutch and demanded a proportionately larger representation in the States-General; the Dutch, thanks to two centuries of national independence, had greater political experience and, on that score, claimed an equal number of deputies. Memories of the past injected their venom into the conflict. The south, until the late sixteenth century, had been the center of culture and political power; now the roles were reversed, and Holland's pre-eminence had to be grudgingly admitted in Antwerp and Brussels.

The language question was a festering sore in the body politic of the new kingdom. In 1823 the king declared the Flemish tongue the official language in the Dutch-speaking provinces, but among the educated classes, who spoke French rather than Flemish, this met with more opposition than support. In 1825 he issued a number of decrees intended to give the state influence over the church, especially over the training of the Catholic clergy. From that moment on the latter showed open hostility to his rule, which became increasingly bitter with the years.

In the Walloon or French-speaking provinces of the south, King William was at first hailed by the liberals, who were more numerous there than in Flanders, but his autocratic tendencies and his disregard of the States-General soon alienated these Walloon progressives. He was bitterly criticized in their papers, whereupon the king's government, in spite of the constitutional guarantee of a free press, proceeded to prosecute the carping editors.

Liberals and Catholics finally banded together to force the king to a change of policy. The Catholics plucked the fruits of that coalition. For the monarch repealed, one after another, the laws that irked them. But this sudden yielding after protracted intransigence did not appease the malcontents. They thought it a sign of weakening and, encouraged by success, piled up their grievances.

There was unrest everywhere in western Europe. Flemish and Walloon discontent was but a spasm of the revolutionary tremor that was running throughout the Continent. As the news of the Three Days' Revolution in Paris, late in July, 1830, traveled north, the trouble came to a head. On the evening of August 25, a new opera, *La Muette de Portici,* had its première in Brussels. The plot was taken from Masaniello's revolt at Naples against Spanish tyranny in 1648. The audience heard their own grievances voiced in the songs of the actors and felt stirred to defiance of King William by Masaniello's defiance of Spain. The Neapolitan scene on the stage became, to their excited vision, their own city of Brussels, and stage acts of revenge were, in a sudden outbreak of fury, re-enacted in the streets outside. The riots spread like wildfire from one town to another until the entire south was in open revolt.

The king, taken aback by the suddenness of the outbreak, steered an unsteady course in the months that followed, veering from attempts at forcible suppression to conciliatory negotiations. When these failed, he addressed an appeal for intervention to the Great Powers that were the guarantors of his rule. But the motives that had prompted them to unite north and south had lost their cogency in 1830. France was no longer a menace to British safety. She had actually been admitted to the coalition, which, through her entrance, had become a quintuple alliance. The powers turned a deaf ear to the king's entreaties, none being anxious to run the risk of war for the sake of healing the breach in William's divided realm. The possibility of reunion was not even considered at the London conference of the Great Powers. They imposed an armistice, proceeded to study the grounds for divorce, and in January, 1831, formulated in a protocol the conditions of separation. These would restore the frontiers of 1792. King William accepted them. But the National Congress, which had been summoned by the provisional government of what was now called Belgium, refused its consent. In the flush of triumph the Belgians insisted on more than was offered them by the Great Powers and these were inclined to meet them halfway, when they found them amenable in another matter that was of greater concern to London. The British government proposed Prince Leopold of Saxe-Coburg, son-in-law of King George IV, as its candidate for the Belgian throne, and when the Belgian Congress elected him king, the powers, in conference at London, revised the terms of separation which they had declared to be irrevocable in favor of the Belgian demands.

It was now King William's turn to reject those conditions, and he notified the foreign ministers of the five powers of his intention "to throw his army into the balance with a view to obtaining more equitable terms of separation." His son and heir, the Prince of Orange, at the head of an army of thirty thousand men, invaded Belgium and completely routed King Leopold's forces in a lightning campaign that lasted only ten days. Intervention by the powers was needed to save Leopold of Saxe-Coburg from losing his new kingdom. A British diplomat arranged an armistice, the powers revised a second time the conditions of separation, and Belgium paid the penalty of defeat by accepting them. On November 15, 1831, the treaty was signed in London by her envoy and the plenipotentiaries of the five great powers, each of which guaranteed the new kingdom's neutrality and inviolability. The final settlement with Holland was postponed, owing to the obstinacy of King William, who felt that his army's military success entitled him to more generous terms. He finally signed the London treaty on February 1, 1839.

The people in the north had stood loyally by their king in these trying days. But their loyalty was a way of demonstrating their condemnation of the Belgian revolt. It was not prompted by approval of his policy and the use he made of the royal power. He had become an absolute monarch by gradually removing all the checks the constitution put upon him. He discarded the Council of State, ruled without responsible ministers, made decisions on the most important matters without the co-operation of the States-General, sought to influence the judiciary and would allow no examination of the inscrutable manner in which he administered the state finances. His most loyal counselors became disaffected. Van Hogendorp, the king maker and the framer of the constitution, who as he grew older became more and more liberal, resigned as vice-president of the Council of State in 1816, and withdrew entirely from active participation in public affairs in 1825. The king, in short, ruled as a despot, and the best that can be said of his reign is that his despotism was of the kind that is called enlightened. He had indeed great qualities: tireless industry, a flair for business, a talent for finance, the courage of initiative, a genuine interest in the education and welfare of the masses. Important institutions that have survived his reign owe their origin to his initiative or sponsorship, among others the Netherlands Bank, a private enterprise, but authorized under its charter to issue Netherlands paper money; the Netherlands Trading Society, founded in 1824 for the express purpose of reviving the lagging carrying trade and the navigation to the East Indies; the *Maatschappij van Weldadigheid,* a charitable society that reclaimed land with a view to relieving poverty; the neutral primary school; and the institution of state universities.

The country had always boasted a transportation system second to none, thanks to its widespread net of canals. It was, consequently, slow in availing itself of the new possibilities that the steam engine offered. But King William had more imagination than most of his subjects. He promoted the building of the first railway from Amsterdam to Haarlem, in spite of opposition, indifference, and ridicule. At the same time the popular *trekschuit,* the horse-drawn canal barge, was superseded by the steamboat, and this again was a development that claimed the king's attention and foresight. He took a hand in the founding of steamship companies in Rotterdam and Amsterdam, and improved the approaches to both ports by the construction of new canals. His vision took in vaster territory than continental Holland. He had ambitious plans for the future of Curaçao, which he hoped to promote with the digging of a canal, by Dutch engineers and at Holland's expense, across Central America.

There were, indeed, few men in Holland who equaled King William I in vision, energy, and business capacity. He rose head and shoulders above the bulk of the nation, not by virtue of the majesty it had conferred upon him, but because of his personal endowments. He ruled a people who seemed hardly worthy of so excellent a king. The popular morale was low. The Napoleonic era had reduced the nation to poverty. To live frugally had become the compelling need of the time. People's minds were preoccupied with the thought of how they could provide for the morrow. They lived from hand to mouth and had no leisure for indulging the cravings of mind and spirit. The general tone of Dutch society was, consequently, low. Its fiction was unimaginative, its poetry either pedestrian or bombastic, science straggled in the track of foreign research, art manufactured soulless academic masterpieces, drama was sentimental drivel, and music was borrowed from abroad.

The people's interest in politics was at an equally low ebb, and this apathy condones, if it does not justify, the king's assumption of arbitrary personal rule. There were as yet no parties with clearly formulated platforms. The prejudices and predilections of the different social strata made up for the lack of party programs. The proletariat, as always, was loyal to the House of Orange. The middle class, especially its higher layers, from which the Patriots had been recruited, remained critical of the royal house, and constituted the progressive element of the nation. The descendants of the eighteenth-century oligarchs, realizing that they could best salvage the remnants of their forefathers' influence and prestige in the shelter of the dynasty, had made their peace with the House of Orange. And the nobility, of course, had no interest in opposing the royal power which was its only mainstay in Holland's bourgeois society.

There was more public interest in church than in state matters. The Reformed Church, in the days of the Republic, had been the training ground of the common burgher in democratic practices. He did not participate in elections for public offices, but he did have a say in the choice of elders and deacons, and indirectly, through these, of the ministers. In 1798 the Reformed Church had lost its privileged status, and the restoration of 1813 had not re-established it. But the rank and file of the people still regarded this as the national church. That, indeed, it was, for it tried to encompass within its fold the most diverse shades of Protestantism by means of a vague and colorless formula. Such latitude would have horrified the ministers of the seventeenth century. Eighteenth-century rationalism, deistic reasoning, and the popularization of scientific discoveries had blunted the sharp edges of Calvinist orthodoxy. The average Dutch churchgoer had become a dull, unzealous, and spiritless performer of his Sunday-morning social duty.

Reaction against this moral decline of the church came from two sides, from a small group of scholars and esthetes at Amsterdam, and from orthodox circles in the rural districts. The Amsterdam group called itself the *Réveil,* a name that, with the ideas it stood for, came from French Switzerland. Its adherents looked upon Willem Bilderdijk as their spiritual father and had a gifted leader in Isaac da Costa, the son of a Portuguese Jewish family whom Bilderdijk had converted to the Reformed religion. They wanted to rekindle the fervor and emotion of old-time Calvinism and bring religious experience back from the head to the heart. Their movement, however, remained restricted to patrician circles, and though it had decided influence on the thought and the literature of the period, the church itself was little affected by it.

The revivalism in the rural districts had more serious results. Zealous Calvinists, under the leadership of their ministers, despairing of the restoration of the national church to its pristine orthodoxy, decided to secede and constitute a new church body. The government refused to recognize the separatists, deprived the leaders of their pulpits, fined participants in their forbidden conventicles, and imprisoned the most recalcitrant. But the king's attempt to subdue the movement was doomed to failure. It grew against oppression, and his son and successor, William II, took the wiser course of leaving them in peace. A potato blight, which ruined the principal food of the country poor, added material distress to the miseries of persecution, and in order to escape both plagues large groups of separatists, under the leadership of their ministers, sailed for America and settled down in the Middle West. Holland, Michigan, founded by the Reverend A. C. van Raalte, and Pella, Iowa, settled by the Reverend H. P. Scholte, owe their origin to this migration.

In 1840 King William I abdicated in favor of his eldest son. He was disillusioned by the failure of his Belgian policy and embittered by the growing opposition in Holland against his autocratic rule. Having been forced by the legislature to concede certain limitations of his royal power, he did not care to retain it with curtailments that were irksome to his pride. He left Holland for an estate that he owned in Silesia, and died in 1843 at Berlin.

Under the rule of his son, William II (1840-49), and his grandson, William III (1849-90), the progressive forces, which derived from the Patriot movement, gathered headway and finally gained predominance. They now went by the name of Liberals, but the new label made them no more acceptable to the dynasty. Both kings showed open hostility to the tenets of Liberalism. Remembering the indignities the House of Orange had endured from the Patriots, they saw in these new radicals a menace to their royal power. They tried to block their progress toward reform with the impediments of a cautious conservatism.

The leader of the Liberals was Jan Rudolf Thorbecke, professor of public law at the University of Leyden. He was the brains and the driving power of the Liberal party. He formulated its principles and defined its aims in terse, eloquent prose. He was a popular lecturer, but does not seem to have possessed the gift of making himself loved by his fellow workers. There was something rigid and awkward in his manner—a residue, perhaps, of his middle-class origin— that gave him a sense of social inferiority, painful to his intellectual pride. But the class from which he sprang had full confidence in his wisdom, and from its midst came the support that he needed to carry his radical proposals through the legislature.

The revolutionary storm that raged over Europe in the forties blew also, though with diminished force, across the political scene of Holland. It swept the Liberals into power in 1848. King William II read the handwriting on the wall and, to ward off revolution at home, gave way to the Liberal opposition. A committee of five Liberals under Thorbecke drafted a new constitution which laid the foundations for the modern democracy that Holland became under Queen Wilhelmina. Its passage marked, indeed, the beginning of a new era. The law itself, of course, did not carry the seeds of the new life, but it thawed the frost of conservatism that had kept those seeds from developing. Thorbecke's constitution brought the liberating spring in whose clement weather new political and social ideas could blossom and bear fruit.

The personal rule of the monarch was abolished, though he still retained extensive power. His ministers were declared responsible for his acts to the States-General. The First Chamber, whose members used to be appointed by the king, were henceforth to be elected by the provincial States, and these, as well as the Second Chamber, would be chosen directly by all persons paying a certain amount in taxation. The legislature was given the right of amending bills submitted, on behalf of the crown, by its responsible ministers. It also obtained the right of passing on the annual budget and scrutinizing the government's expenditures. And the king's personal administration of the colonies was curtailed by the right of the States-General to have a say in their management.

During the reign of King William III (1849-90) the people's right to self-government was gradually extended and reinforced, in spite of the monarch's reluctance to yield to Liberal pressure. The rise of a militant Liberal party induced its opponents to organize and formulate principles and aims in their turn. Hence Dutch political life became clearly patterned and variegated. The conservatives were recruited from the orthodox Calvinists and assumed the name of Antirevolutionaries. They proclaimed by that label that they were opposed to the rationalism of the eighteenth century which had produced the French Revolution and to contemporary Liberalism in which they saw a modern offshoot of that damnable creed. Groen van Prinsterer, one of the leaders of Da Costa's *Réveil,* was the intellectual sponsor of this movement. But he died before the party was actually constituted. Its first leader was Dr. Abraham Kuyper, a man of great versatility, theologian, journalist, statesman and powerful orator. But his many-sidedness caused disunion within the party. He could not keep his political and church activities apart. They were to him identical interests. But there were many among his followers who wanted to abide by the synodal institutions and the state universities, both of which Kuyper bitterly attacked. In 1880 he founded at Amsterdam the Free University on Reformed Principles; in 1886 he left the national church and established his own, the Suffering Church, as he called it. These steps alienated the more conservative and patrician elements among the Antirevolutionaries. They left his leadership and called their secession the Christian Historical party. The bulk of Kuyper's following belonged to the lower middle class. He liked to refer to himself as the leader of the *kleine luiden,* "the small people," and to the aristocrats of the Christian Historical party as "the gentlemen with double names." As a theologian he was a conservative, as a politician and social reformer he was a radical who out-liberaled the Liberals.

The Catholics also came to the fore as a distinct political entity. Thorbecke proposed, in 1853, to give them freedom of organization as guaranteed under the constitution of that year, and the measure was carried over the violent protests of the ministers of the Dutch Reformed Church. Hence, in the first years of their existence as a party, the Catholics usually sided with the Liberals. But their union was short-lived. The neutral public school, the special pet of Liberalism, was assailed by both Calvinists and Catholics. Their common fight for the Christian school brought the two together. Kuyper did not find it easy to overcome his Calvinist followers' distrust of what their seventeenth-century ancestors used to call popery. But his great prestige and his power of persuasion won their consent to a coalition with the Catholic party. "As faithful Calvinists," he told them, "you ought to oppose Rome in all dogmatic and religious matters, but to reckon on their support if you find them willing to fight for your Christian school and for the Christian foundation of the state."

The Centre, as the Catholic party was called, was not a negligible ally. Foreigners think of Holland as a Protestant state. It was that in the days of the Dutch Republic, when Catholic citizens had no right to public worship and the provinces of North Brabant and Limburg, which are solidly Catholic, were not members of the Union but were treated as conquered territories wrested from Spanish rule after the Union of Utrecht had been signed. But under the monarchy these provinces were given equal status with the others, and when Catholics ceased to be treated as second-class citizens, they became a political power in the land. For they constitute thirty-five per cent of the country's population, and since the clergy sees to it that the Catholic voter does not neglect his duty as a citizen and all schismatic tendencies within the party are suppressed, the Centre usually casts a ballot that is fairly representative of its voting strength, whereas the other parties always suffer from defections and secessions.

Schism occurred, as we saw, in Kuyper's party; it also happened in Thorbecke's. Progressives and conservatives drifted away from each other. Thorbecke, as he grew older, lost his ardor for progressive reform. There were radical elements among his followers who opposed his doctrine that the state must abstain as much as possible from interfering with the economic life of its citizens. Old-fashioned Liberalism believed that, if production throve, thanks to the elimination of all obstacles to the free flow of commerce, distribution would follow automatically, and that prosperity at the top would gradually spread among the lower layers of society. But an official investigation begun in 1886 revealed that many workers in both commerce and industry were living on the edge of pauperism, that housing conditions were appalling, that wages were low, and the working hours too long. These revelations gave the lie to the optimism of the Thorbeckean Liberals, and brought grist to the mill of the radicals. The party finally split into three factions, in the late nineties, owing to the secession of the conservatives and of the radical wing.

But meanwhile, thanks to the gradual extension of the suffrage, the laboring class became politically articulate. The industrial revolution, which had concentrated production in a small number of large factories, had worked a profound change in the relationship between master and servant. In the small workshops of earlier days the boss plied his tools together with his assistants and did not feel himself the latter's social superior. But in the large industrial plants that gradually put the workshops of individual craftsmen out of business, the employer became estranged from his personnel, and the cleavage between capital and labor became accentuated. An industrial proletariat arose whose discontent listened eagerly to the preaching of the war of classes.

The coalition of Calvinists and Catholics, the rise of labor as a political factor, and the centrifugal forces at work within the Liberal party weakened the predominant position that Liberalism had maintained during the seventies and eighties. It is in the nature of Liberalism to set free the very forces that threaten to become its undoing. For it would have been untrue to itself if it had not created that broader knowledge and that liberty of action which made it possible for Catholics, orthodox Calvinists, and proletarians to develop their political parties. These were the forces that were destined to defeat and dethrone Liberalism in the early years of the twentieth century.

Not least among the many achievements that the Liberals had to their credit was the reform they effected in the administration of the colonies. That administration was hardly ever a subject of public debate before Thorbecke came into power. Before 1800 the government of the Indies had been the concern of the East India Company. Its charter was revoked in 1798, and its assets and liabilities were taken over by the Batavian Republic. But state management did not last long enough to make the Dutch people colony minded. When Holland was incorporated with the Napoleonic Empire, Great Britain seized the Dutch possessions in the Malay Archipelago on the ground that they were now enemy territory. Sir Thomas Stamford Raffles was made lieutenant governor of Java, and during his brief rule (1811–16) he tried to strengthen and perfect the administrative machine along the lines of policy inaugurated by his Dutch predecessor Daendels.

His new English broom did some vigorous sweeping at the outset, but gradually the inertia of routine and tradition forced him back into the rut of the Dutch East India Company's policies. The merit of his rule was not in what he achieved but in what he envisaged, and as a pioneer who pointed the way toward a better colonial practice, he occupies a place of honor in the gallery of East Indian administrators.

Sir Thomas saw in the native rulers, quite justifiably, the chief oppressors of the common people, and in order to destroy the feudal system which was the basis of their power he abolished their hereditary right to succession and made them salaried appointees, charged with the administration of their districts under the strict supervision of European governors—the residents so called. Lacking funds, however, to pay them their salaries, Sir Thomas resorted to payments in land, a device by which he restored the very feudalism that he was bent on destroying. For the natives who occupied these lands automatically, if not willingly, resumed the time-honored deliveries in kind to which the feudal lords had always been entitled.

In 1816 Great Britain returned the islands to the new kingdom of the Netherlands. The necessity of giving economic strength to England's sentry on the northern frontier of France prompted the government in London to this act of generosity. The Dutch controlled, at that time, only a small part of the island territory they now possess. Even Java was not yet entirely theirs, and outside Java their power extended to the Moluccas, to the Minahassa in North Celebes, and to a few towns on the coasts of Borneo and Sumatra. Hence the expansion of Holland's colonial empire was largely accomplished in the nineteenth century.

Great changes took place during that period, not only in Holland's political position in the Far East, but also in her conceptions of the rights and duties of a colonial power. Until 1877 the native labor of Java was employed to produce wealth under a system of forced cultivation. Instead of paying to the government, as formerly, a certain proportion of their crops—two-fifths of the harvest under Raffles—the Javanese were required to place at the government's disposal a certain proportion of their land and one-fifth of their labor time. The advantage of this system was that the government could prescribe what kinds of crops should be cultivated, instead of having to accept the rice the natives grew to the exclusion of nearly everything else.

In theory it was not a bad plan, for it encouraged experimentation with new crops. But in practice it did not work so well. It discouraged private enterprise, the officials strove to distinguish themselves by stimulating production and bringing in revenue, and as a result the natives were overworked and underpaid. The system was introduced in the early thirties by Governor General Johannes van den Bosch (1830–34). It produced big profits and enabled King William I to stabilize Holland's badly shaken finances. Since the administration of the colonies was held to be his personal concern, the Dutch public was kept in ignorance of conditions in Java. But the revised constitution of 1848 gave Parliament some control of colonial affairs, and from then on a growing minority in the Second Chamber insisted on abandonment of the system. The East India Government Act of 1854 brought some reform, but not yet the necessary protection for the native workers against exploitation by the government. Public opinion was aroused, at last, by the publication of *Max Havelaar,* an autobiographic novel by Multatuli, pen name of Edward Douwes Dekker, a discharged colonial official, who exposed with biting sarcasm the evils of this revenue-producing agriculture by means of forced labor. Under pressure of a growing demand for sharper parliamentary supervision of the colonial administration, the legislature in

1870 passed the Agrarian Law which paved the way for the gradual abandonment of the wicked system.

It was superseded by one of private exploitation. Wild lands were leased to Europeans and reclaimed for cultivation by hired native labor, and the government assumed the role of guardian of the native workers. According to the theory promulgated in 1870 the government is the owner of all land, but it holds it as a trustee for the actual owner, the native tiller of the soil, whom it protects against exploitation and his own gullibility. In practice, therefore, all arable land is the inalienable property of the native people, so that no foreigner, be he European or Arab or Chinese, can obtain property rights to any lands for agricultural purposes. The Dutch sugar planter who needs irrigated rice fields for the cultivation of his crop must rent them from the Javanese owners. All leases must be passed before government officials, and these see to it that no contract calls for more land than the natives can spare.

The government revenue, formerly obtained by the sale of compulsorily grown crops, was now collected in the form of taxes, levied on both the European planters and the native population. The poll tax for natives was not felt to be an injustice. It simply took the place of the traditional *heerendiensten* or services rendered in labor by subjects to their overlord. Still, direct taxation proved unpopular with the natives; they much preferred to pay in an indirect way. In accordance with their wishes, the poll tax was finally abolished in 1927. They continued to pay a land tax, the amount of which was based partly on the area and partly on the value of its produce. But they contributed more to the treasury through indirect duties on various necessaries of life.

The old discontent died down, thanks to the tactful methods of the Dutch officials and to the people's realization of the fact that the government was trying its honest best to divide the burden with even justice. They knew, besides, that the revenue collected was spent on the administration of their islands, on the maintenance of public order, the improvement of roads, the dispensation of justice, on irrigation, public health, schools, and various other benefits that western rule had brought them. For after the year 1877 no East Indian surpluses were used for the benefit of the Netherlands treasury.

The gradual extension of Dutch rule over the entire archipelago was chiefly a process of peaceful penetration. The native rulers were persuaded to recognize Netherlands sovereignty in return for an undertaking on the part of the Dutch government that it would maintain them in power. From the earliest days of Dutch occupation of the islands, the Hollanders have followed a policy of noninterference in the internal affairs of the native states. Only where the princes proved a danger to Netherlands sovereignty did the government step in. Hence there are two kinds of territory, the indirectly governed states, and those under direct Dutch rule. Only seven per cent of Java is indirectly ruled, but in more than half the area of the other islands native princes are still in control under the sovereignty of the government in Batavia.

Serious trouble was encountered only in the sultanate of Atjeh, in North Sumatra. In 1824 the Dutch government had concluded a treaty with Great Britain under which Holland waived all claims to the Malaccan Peninsula and England withdrew from the island of Sumatra, on condition, however, that the Dutch government should maintain safety of navigation along the Atjeh coasts and should respect Atjeh's independence. But the Dutch soon discovered that it was impossible to police the sea and maintain a hands-off policy toward the sultanate, whose ruler derived no inconsiderable part of his revenue from the piratical expeditions of his subjects. In the year 1831 an American ship was looted by Atjehnese, and the Dutch government, its hands tied by the treaty with England, left it to the United States to send a punitive expedition. In 1871, however, Holland was released by Great Britain from the irksome obligation to respect Atjeh's integrity. The sultan, scenting trouble, tried to play a double game, negotiating with the government at Batavia about a *modus vivendi*, while secretly applying for help to France, Italy, and the United States. An ultimatum was handed to him, demanding an explanation of his double-dealing and recognition of Netherlands suzerainty. When both were refused, war was declared on March 26, 1873. It lasted for nearly forty years. In 1910 the last spasms of resistance ceased, and a new era of peaceful penetration was inaugurated.

The Hollanders had gone to the Indies as traders. Commerce, not conquest, was their aim. It was by the compulsion of circumstances, and almost against their own will, that they became rulers over an island realm vastly larger than their own little country. They were long guilty of selfish exploitation of its natural resources and native labor. But under Liberal leadership in the sixties and seventies of the past century they awoke to a realization of the duties and responsibilities that their possession of these islands involved. And after the trend toward reform had once started, its progress gained impetus from the accumulating evidence of its beneficial effects. At the opening of the twentieth century the stage was set for profound changes in the political and economic framework of the Indies, which were to prepare the natives for active participation in the government under Netherlands guardianship.

CHAPTER XI

The Age of Wilhelmina

QUEEN WILHELMINA was the daughter of King William III's second marriage, the child of his old age. At ten she inherited his titles and dignities, as the three sons from his first union had all preceded their father in death. Her mother, Queen Emma, acted as regent during her minority. On September 6, 1898, the young queen was sworn in and inaugurated, in a joint meeting of the First and Second Chambers, held in the New Church at Amsterdam.

She assumed the reins of government at an auspicious moment. The nation had fully awakened from its lethargy. With all the social layers contributing their energy as never before to the national effort, Holland had begun to unfold a fresh activity both in Europe and in her overseas territories. Her commerce was expanding, new industries were springing up, a note of self-confidence was struck in her literature, musical production reached a high standard, Dutch painting was finding new ways of expression, Dutch stagecraft was raised from mere entertainment to an art, and Holland's architects were creating an original style that gave fresh beauty to her fine old cities.

The ideas that Liberalism stood for had, at the beginning of Wilhelmina's reign, become the common heritage of all. This does not mean to imply that party divisions had ceased to exist, but it cannot be denied that the individual Hollander, whatever his political allegiance, was a Liberal in thought. Reactionary opinions might still be harbored by conservative landowners and some old-time aristocrats of the Christian Historical party; but the large majority of both Calvinists and Catholics were progressive and at one with the Liberals on plans for social betterment and reform. The workers' right to protection against the effects of disability, disease, and old age was widely recognized, and proposals for various legislative enactments that would guarantee freedom from want to all citizens met with slight opposition from any party. The objections raised were not prompted by any desire to deny that right, but by a theoretical aversion to all state interference in the private lives of its citizens. Such meddling, it was argued, would blunt the sense of individual responsibility and substitute the heartless, because impersonal, provision of the state for the ministrations of private charity.

There was, no doubt, some ground for misgivings on that score. But the industrial revolution had greatly increased the number of accidents and the prevalence of occupational diseases. It was realized that private initiative alone could no longer cope with modern conditions. And thus, after long debates and repeated revisions of the original draft, legislation was enacted, under the sponsorship of a coalition cabinet of Calvinists and Catholics, which provided for compulsory insurance of the worker against disability, and for state pensions for the aged, widows, and orphans.

The rise of a strong Labor party and the organization of the workers in labor unions gave them an added sense of security and political prestige. The party's growth, under the leadership of P. J. Troelstra, in the first two decades of this century, was phenomenal. In 1897 the Socialist vote was only 13,500. In 1901 that figure rose to 40,585, and in 1913 it jumped to more than 145,000. Not all these votes, indeed, came from party members. Radicals in the Liberal camp were apt to give their support to labor candidates, though they did not subscribe to the revolutionary slogans of socialism. They took these with a grain of salt, since Troelstra's party had purged itself, in 1909, of the extreme elements in its midst. The latter, after their expulsion, founded a Communist party which prided itself on its Marxian orthodoxy, while the Labor party showed a growing inclination to support the monarchy under the House of Orange rather than agitate for a Red republic. Troelstra, carried away, in 1918, by the success of his German comrades Ebert and Scheidemann, made an attempt at revolution, but his fellow leaders disavowed him and steered the party away from the path of violence. This moderation had beneficial results for the industrial workers, as it rallied to labor's fight for economic security wider support from the other parties than an intransigent Marxism could have obtained. Thanks to that aid the menace of unemployment lost its terror. The trade unions were enabled to insure their members with partial support of the government. Besides, an Unemployment Council was set up, in which the various agencies for the care of the jobless had their central organ.

Housing conditions, too, were greatly improved. Thanks to state subsidies for the construction and upkeep of new homes in place of slum dwellings declared unfit for habitation, the industrial centers were enabled to lease them to low-wage earners at reduced rentals. Amsterdam took the lead in this campaign. By enlisting the services of H. P. Berlage, the country's greatest architect and town planner, the city erected on its outskirts artistic group dwellings where the laboring classes could live in comfortable homes, well aired, well lighted, and an esthetic pleasure to the eye. This example was followed in many other cities, and even in rural areas. Berlage and his followers changed not only the aspect of town and country, but also the attitude of town and country dwellers toward their environment.

Thus the amenities of life were brought within the reach of ever larger numbers. And a steadily widening distribution

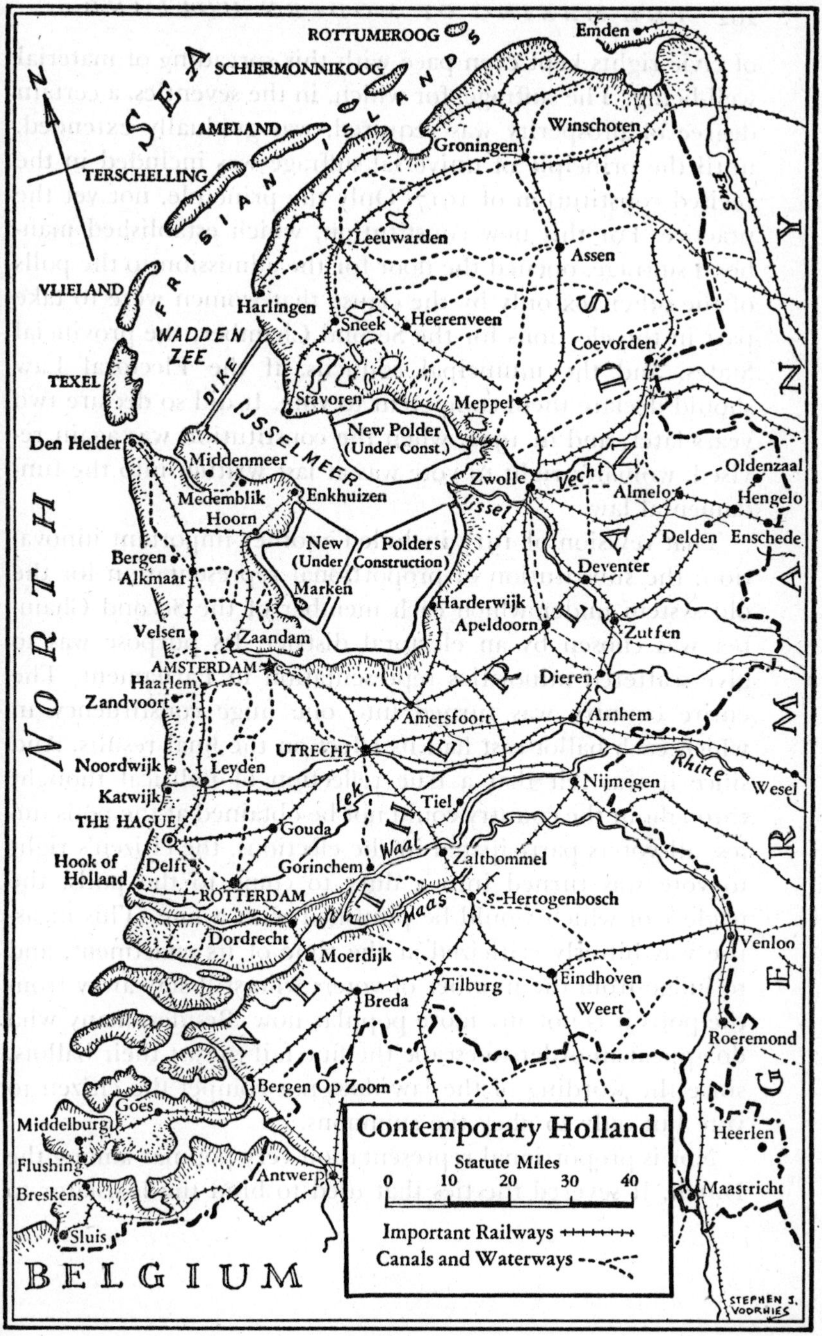
Contemporary Holland
Statute Miles
0 10 20 30 40
Important Railways
Canals and Waterways
NORTH SEA
FRISIAN ISLANDS
ROTTUMEROOG
SCHIERMONNIKOOG
AMELAND
TERSCHELLING
VLIELAND
TEXEL
WADDEN ZEE
DIKE
IJSSELMEER
New Polder (Under Const.)
New Polders (Under Construction)
Emden
Winschoten
Groningen
EMS
Leeuwarden
Assen
Harlingen
Sneek
Heerenveen
Coevorden
Stavoren
Meppel
Den Helder
Middenmeer
Medemblik
Enkhuizen
Zwolle
Vecht
Ijssel
Oldenzaal
Almelo
Hengelo
Hoorn
Delden
Enschede
Bergen
Alkmaar
Marken
Deventer
Harderwijk
Apeldoorn
Zutfen
Velsen
Zaandam
AMSTERDAM
Haarlem
Dieren
Zandvoort
Amersfoort
Arnhem
UTRECHT
Rhine
Noordwijk
Leyden
Nijmegen
Wesel
Katwijk
Lek
Tiel
THE HAGUE
Gouda
Waal
Hook of Holland
Delft
Gorinchem
Zaltbommel
ROTTERDAM
Maas
's-Hertogenbosch
Dordrecht
Moerdijk
Venloo
Tilburg
Eindhoven
Breda
Weert
Roeremond
Bergen Op Zoom
Goes
Middelburg
Heerlen
Flushing
Antwerp
Maastricht
Breskens
Sluis
BELGIUM
GERMANY
THE NETHERLANDS
STEPHEN J. VOORHIES

of civic rights kept even pace with this spreading of material well-being. The suffrage, for which, in the seventies, a certain degree of prosperity was required, was gradually extended, until the principle of universal suffrage was included in the revised constitution of 1917. Only the principle, not yet the practice. For this new constitution, which established manhood suffrage, opened the door for the admission to the polls of the other sex only by the clause that women were to take part in the elections for the Second Chamber, the provincial States, and the municipal councils, if the Electoral Law should declare them competent to vote. It did so declare two years later, and in 1922, when the constitution was again revised, woman's right to vote was at last written into the fundamental law.

That revision of 1917 included another important innovation: the substitution of proportional representation for the old system under which each member of the Second Chamber was chosen by an electoral district. Its purpose was to give scattered minorities representation in Parliament. The entire country was turned into one huge constituency in which each ballot cast had its effect on the final results. And since it was felt that a true reflection of political thought throughout the country could not be obtained at the polls unless all voters participated in the elections, the citizen's right to vote was turned into a duty to come to the polls, the neglect of which would be punished with a fine. This measure was bitterly criticized at the time of its enactment, and to judge from the number of voters who still stay away from the polls it is not any more popular now. Besides, many who do appear in order to escape the fine fail to cast their ballots, since the wording of the law does not compel the citizen to vote but only to obey the summons.

Nor is proportional representation very popular among the Dutch. It severed the ties that used to bind the legislator to the electoral district that returned him; it increased the power of the party bosses; and it produced a prolific crop of little parties that had no political ax to grind but represented the interests of social cliques and professions.

The passage of universal suffrage was secured by a political compromise. The coalition of Calvinists and Catholics gave its consent to that measure in return for recognition by the parties of the left of the equality of public and private education. "Education is an object of the Government's continuous care," Article 192 of the new constitution declared. Exclusive solicitude for public instruction was no longer an explicit maxim of state. The costs of primary education would in future be defrayed from the public revenue, no matter whether it were given in private or in public schools, and subsidies would be granted to private institutions for secondary and higher education on conditions to be fixed by law.

The ministry that sponsored these legislative measures was an extraparliamentary cabinet (1913–18), whose members were independent of the parties represented in the Second Chamber. The left had won the elections, but the left was a coalition of Liberals of various shades with Troelstra's Labor party, and since Troelstra, obedient to the International which forbade Socialist participation in a bourgeois government, declined to accept a cabinet post, the Liberal leaders refused to shoulder responsibility of which the Socialists did not take their due share. In this dilemma the queen invited Mr. Cort van der Linden, who had no affiliation with any party, to form a cabinet, and he, being politically free in the choice of his associates, gathered around himself a group of the most eminent men in their respective professions. Jonkheer J. Loudon, one of Holland's most distinguished diplomats, took charge of the Foreign Office; Dr. M. W. F. Treub, one of her foremost economists, became minister of agriculture, commerce, and industry; and Dr. C. Lely, a hydraulic engineer of European fame, headed the Department of Waterways.

This was in June, 1913. The international outlook was dark at the time. During the first decade of the century relations between Germany and France had become strained. All Europe lived under an obsession that war might break out at any time. The Peace Conference of 1899 at The Hague, for which Czar Nicholas II had taken the initiative, had raised false hopes of a better world in which, to quote the Czar's own words, "the great idea of universal peace would triumph over the elements of trouble and discord." It was actually the other way around: the elements of trouble and discord triumphed over the great idea of universal peace. Three months after the conference closed, the South African War broke out (1899-1902); then followed the Boxer Rebellion in China and the international expedition under von Waldersee (1900), the conflict between Russia and Japan (1904-5), the Kaiser's demonstrative visit to Tangier in 1905, and the crisis following the annexation of Bosnia by Austria (1908). The second Peace Conference of 1907, again held at The Hague, was attended by an imposing number of states, forty-five in all, but they spent more time on considering means to make war more humane than on drafting plans for its prevention.

The government took warning from these ominous signs. Mr. H. Colijn, minister of war in the clerical coalition cabinet of Mr. Th. Heemskerk (1908-13), carried through a thorough reorganization of the army which gave the country a militia sufficiently strong to muster, at the menace of war, 200,000 men for the protection of Holland's neutrality.

Early in August, 1914, this army was mobilized for that very purpose. Still it seemed insufficient for its hazardous task. Under pressure of public opinion, the then minister of war proposed a bill that provided for the gradual mobilization of the *Landstorm,* a second reserve force of volunteers, which gave the commander in chief, in course of time, the disposal of 450,000 trained soldiers.

The war alarm of those early August days was repeated three times in the four years that the World War lasted. The country remained on the alert. The German general staff, no doubt, saw greater advantage in a neutral Holland than in a Holland aligned against the Reich on the side of the Allies. But Germany's reasons for respecting the country's neutrality could gain or lose in force by Holland's own attitude, and Holland could strengthen them by showing a firm front against either group of belligerents. Whatever the failings of the government in the trials of this period, it cannot be accused of ever having used international law as a disguise for an unneutral action. Its interpretation of it may have been open to attack; its appeal to it was never open to suspicion. The powers at war could not afford to let the rules of international law interfere with operations in which their very existence was at stake. Holland, which was often the victim of these infringements, had no means of fighting back other than argument and reasoned protest. Those were the weapons that Minister Loudon wielded, with skill and ingenuity, in his numerous diplomatic notes. With these he championed, not only the justice of his country's course, but the principles of international law itself.

While Germany was seizing other peoples' lands for *Lebensraum,* Holland made plans to create living space for her surplus population. On June 14, 1918, a bill for the enclosure and reclamation of the Zuider Zee, according to the plans of Dr. C. Lely, was unanimously passed by both chambers. Four new polders would be added to the country's territory, which would offer employment to 200,000 people. Work on the outer dike which would close off the North Sea was begun in 1920. Its completion turned the Zuider Zee into an inland lake, part of which will be left undrained so as to serve as a fresh-water reservoir for the adjoining provinces.

In the early fifties of the past century Haarlem Lake was reclaimed, and opened up for colonization. Colonists were invited in and left to shift for themselves. Many drifted in who were unfit and inexperienced. The mortality among them was high, and the disheartened fled the scene of their misfortunes, impoverished and broken in health. Only the hardiest and the most skilled remained to fight it out with nature, and bred a sturdy race of expert farmers. In the new Zuider Zee polders, on the other hand, nothing was left to chance. Scientific planning and guidance by government experts saved the settlers from disillusion and failure.

Holland passed through a difficult period after the signing of the Armistice. Her refusal to extradite the fugitive Kaiser made her unpopular with the Entente. Certain elements in Belgium, feeling confident that the Great Powers would support their ally against the neutral, demanded annexation of Dutch territory which was essential, they claimed, to the future safety of their country. The joint control of navigation on the Scheldt by the two kingdoms was also attacked in Antwerp and Brussels. However, these differences did not lead to lasting hostility. They were gradually ironed out by patiently conducted negotiations, and a settlement satisfactory to both parties was on its way when war broke out.

The country's relation to the rest of the European community, especially in regard to matters of commerce, called for the steady attention of the government. It goes without saying that relations with the German Republic, Holland's greatest customer on the Continent, were of particular concern. From a purely economic point of view a prosperous hinterland, including a prosperous Germany, is important to Dutch prosperity. The rise of Rotterdam to one of the chief ports of the Continent was due to its transit activities, which brought about the transfer of large amounts of overseas goods to the most remote corners of Europe.

After Hitler's rise to power, the aspect of world trade in general and of European trade in particular changed completely. Holland did not escape the impacts of this change. Under the cloak of making Germany self-sufficient, Hitler began his policy of looting the surrounding countries—a looting he could carry out completely only when he had these countries under his political control. Exporters in non-German countries were allured by the high prices the Germans were willing to pay for their products when Germany needed them to build up her war machine. Holland was among the first countries to resist this tendency, and from 1934 on exercised strict control over her exports to Germany, so as to keep them from running out of hand and creating debts that every Dutchman knew the Germans would never be able or willing to meet.

When other trade channels became choked as a result of the world-wide depression, outlets had to be sought for Dutch products. To a great extent these were found on the British market, notwithstanding the rise of British protectionism after 1931 and the Ottawa Agreements of 1932, and at the outbreak of World War II, the United Kingdom had outranked Germany as Holland's principal market. Besides, Holland tried, in collaboration with Belgium and the Scandinavian countries, to agree on certain principles for lowering trade barriers. The Oslo Convention, embodying these principles, gave but slight relief to its partners; not more than fifteen per cent of Holland's trade was carried on with these countries, and furthermore, no move for the lowering of trade barriers could be carried out successfully without the willing co-operation of the Great Powers.

As a result of the stagnation of commerce, unemployment spread throughout the country. The devaluation of the pound and the dollar made matters worse. Pressure from various quarters was brought to bear upon the clerical coalition cabinet of Dr. Colijn to try devaluation as a remedy. But Colijn was stubbornly determined to keep the guilder intact. He trusted to deflation as the safest means of helping the country to weather the world depression. The living standard, he maintained, must be adjusted to the lowered national income. The intact guilder, still on gold and at its prewar parity, was to him a symbol of Dutch independence.

Holland carried on this policy of deflation for exactly five years after the depreciation of sterling. She was last among the nations of the world to abandon the gold standard. When this measure finally was taken on September 25, 1936, it was hailed by all exporters who had to compete in the world market with foreign rivals whose lowered currencies enabled them to undersell Holland's high-priced products.

Although the Netherlands East Indies had by stringent measures succeeded to a very great extent in bringing production costs into line with the gold value of the guilder, their guilder was lowered to the same value as the Netherlands guilder, a measure which of course increased the guilder value of all exports from the Indies.

When, owing to this process of readjustment, salaries dropped by thirty per cent below the 1930 level and Java's plantation workers saw their daily wage decreased from fifty to fifteen guilder cents, the rapidly growing volume of cheap imports from Japan proved a real blessing. They made life easier for both Europeans and natives. But this temporary relief did not blind the Dutch to the danger involved in Japan's economic expansion. One of the chief concerns of the East Indies as an agrarian export region was improvement of the trade balance with Japan. In 1934 Japan's purchases in the Indies amounted to no more than nineteen million guilders, whereas she sold to them for a value of ninety-three million. Java sugar, which in the twenties made up fifty per cent of the entire exports of the island, was prac-

The Netherlands East Indies

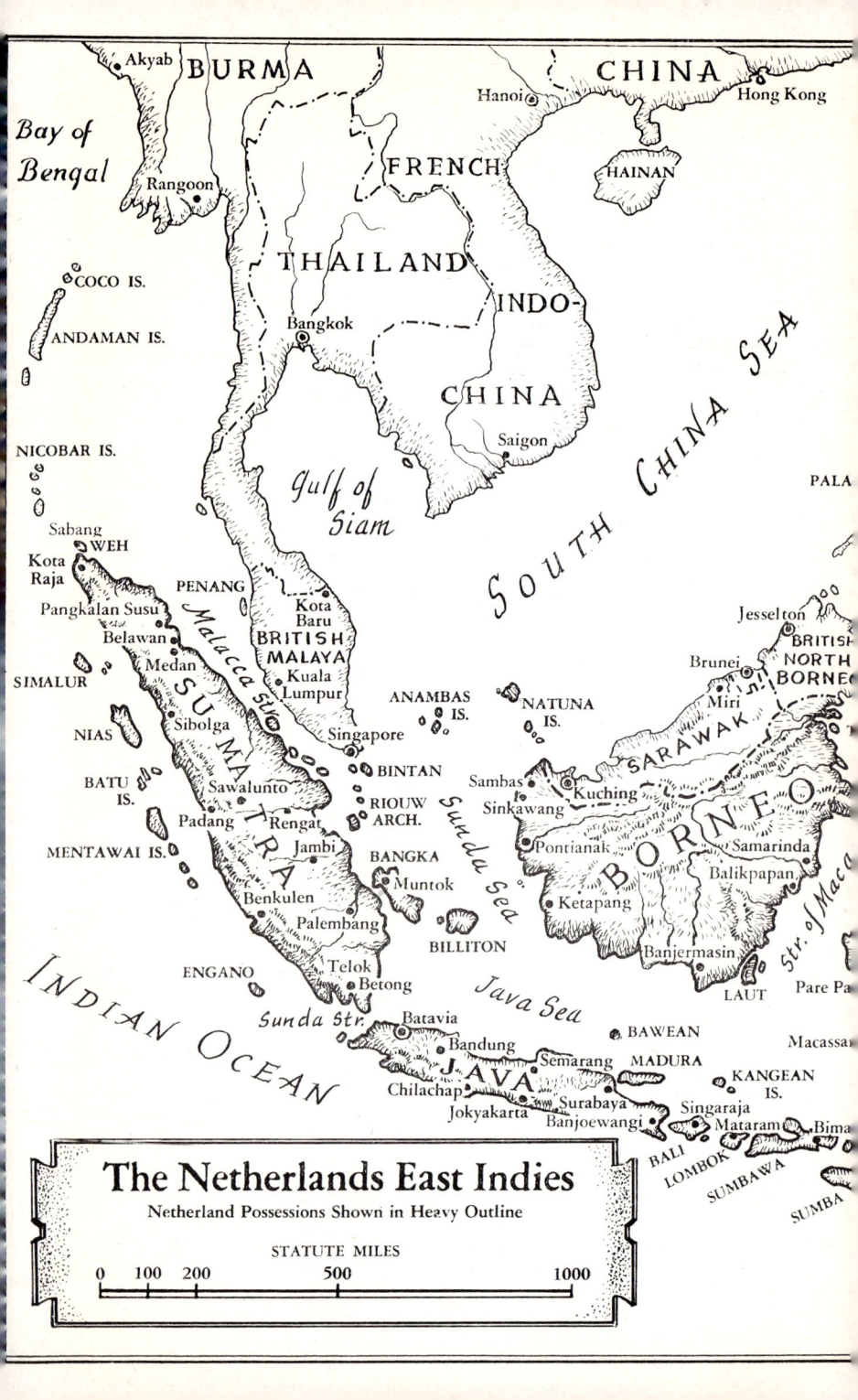

Netherland Possessions Shown in Heavy Outline

STATUTE MILES
0 — 100 — 200 — 500 — 1000

TAIWAN
MARIANAS ISLANDS
SAIPAN
TINIAN
GUAM
PACIFIC OCEAN
Vigan
LUZON
Manila
PHILIPPINE ISLANDS
MINDORA
MASBATE
SAMAR
PANAY
LEYTE
CEBU
NEGROS
BOHOL
MINDANAO
Davao
SULU ARCH.
ULITHI IS.
FAIS
CAROLINE ISLANDS
WOLEAI
YAP
SOROL
PALAU IS.
SONSORAL
PULO ANNA
TALAUD IS.
TOBI
Celebes Sea
SANGI IS.
Passage
MOROTAI
Menado
Ternate
HALMAHERA
Kuandang
Gorontalo
TIDORE
Molucca
BACHAN IS.
MOLUCCAS
WAIGEO
SCHOUTEN IS.
Manokwari
Sorong
Mataboor
Hollandia
Aitape
SULA IS.
OBI IS.
MISOL
Ceram Sea
Fak Fak
NEW GUINEA
DUTCH
BRITISH
Kolonodale
CERAM
BURU
AMBOINA
Kendari
Banda Sea
Dobo
ARU IS.
KEI IS.
MUNA
BUTON
Baubau
FREDERIK HENDRIK IS.
Merauke
TANIMBAR IS.
WETAR
ALOR
Dili
Portugal
Ende
Dutch
TIMOR
Kupang
ROTI
Torres Strait
Arafura Sea
MELVILLE
BATHURST
WESEL IS.
Darwin
Timor Sea
AUSTRALIA
STEPHEN J. VOORHIES

tically excluded from Japan, whose own sugar plantations in Formosa had begun to supply more than her needs. Hence, since expansion of Java's export trade to Japan was not feasible, the proper balance between exports and imports had to be attained by restriction of Japan's imports and by the development of native industries, which, thanks to the cheapness of Javanese labor, would be able to compete with manufactures from Japan. Holland entered reluctantly upon a policy of trade restriction by means of quotas. It was a departure from her free-trade policy of the open door, which she had consistently maintained until the depression period forced her to change her course.

Another issue between Tokyo and Batavia was the rivalry between Japanese and Dutch shipping. The Dutch had taken the initiative for the establishment of a direct shipping line between the Netherlands East Indies and Japan in 1903. With the expansion of trade two, and later three, Japanese lines established steamship connections of their own with the Indies, joining in the aggressive policy of trying to build up a continuous "all-Japanese-chain" from factory to retail sale.

The Netherlands East Indies government was thereby forced to take countermeasures. In an effort to come to an understanding the Netherlands shipping interests sent a delegation to Kobe at the end of 1934, which failed to achieve anything, owing to Japanese insistence that the only language permissible in the conference be Japanese. However, at a conference in Batavia in 1936, an agreement was arrived at which lasted until the outbreak of hostilities.

Gradually it became clear that Japan was preparing for forcible seizure of the islands and their inclusion in the coprosperity sphere her statesmen envisaged. The government at Batavia, therefore, well aware that war could not be avoided, did not hesitate to shoulder its part of the gigantic task of resisting Japanese aggression. Immediately after Pearl Harbor, even before the President of the United States proclaimed that a state of war existed between this country and Japan, the Netherlands government in exile and the government of the Dutch East Indies declared war on Hirohito's empire.

The Japanese invasion demolished the carefully built substructure of an autonomous Indonesian administration. Its first stone was laid in 1903, when a law was passed for the decentralization of administrative functions in Java and other sufficiently developed parts of the archipelago. Local and provincial self-governing bodies were set up, which gave the people an opportunity to take part, through their spokesmen, in the government of provinces, districts, and towns. The principle of self-rule thus established was, subsequently, extended to the central government. By an act of December 16, 1916, a *Volksraad* or People's Council was set up, which has consisted since 1925 of sixty-one members, including the president, twenty-five of whom are Hollanders, thirty natives, and five foreign Orientals. The ordinances passed by the *Volksraad* form the basis of Indonesian legislation. At its incipience the council was merely an advisory board that had to be consulted by the governor general on certain specified subjects, but the Administration Act of 1925 expanded its powers to such an extent that the islands had a fair measure of legislative autonomy. Budgets of the expenses and revenues of the Indies were fixed by the *Volksraad* though subject to approval by the Netherlands legislature. This meant that the *Volksraad* exercised, in addition to its legislative prerogative, a fairly large amount of control in financial and executive matters. Subject to this control the executive functions remained the task of the governor general, who relied for advice on the *Raad van Indië,* or Council of the Indies, and for aid on the heads of the nine Departments of General Administration, which together formed a Council of Department Heads. But in the composition of the executive organs the association of increasing numbers of Indonesians has been one of the most important and consistent aims. Even the highest positions are open to them.

Slowly but securely, during the thirties, the structure of self-rule was perfected on this foundation. The appointment of a Javanese prince to Her Majesty's Cabinet of Ministers in the early summer of 1942 was a logical consequence of the principles that had guided the Dutch government since the early twentieth century. Participation of Indonesians in the Indies government had become a matter of course in the succeeding decades. Several of the highest positions under the governor general were held by natives. But never before did a Javanese hold office in the government of the home country. The inclusion of Pangeran Ario Suyono in Her Majesty's cabinet in London was, therefore, an event of more than passing significance. It foreshadowed a postwar Netherlands commonwealth comprising four coequal units—Holland, the East Indies, Surinam, and Curaçao, which would be independent in internal affairs but united in readiness to render mutual assistance.

The coherence of that realm was strengthened during Wilhelmina's reign through radiotelephone and aviation. The first flights from Amsterdam to Batavia, in the twenties, took from twelve to fifteen days. Ten years later the flying time had been reduced to one hundred hours. The ninety-eight hundred miles that separate Java from Holland became an insignificant barrier. In the late thirties, three-day flights twice a week brought the Indies so much closer to Holland that Dutchmen who never used to give a thought to Java had East Indian affairs thrust upon their attention from day to day. The days when the Dutch public lived in ignorance of what happened in the colonies were over. The very name of colonies had become obsolete. It was deleted from the constitution in the revision of 1922. Wherever it occurred in the text of 1887 it was replaced by the names of the territories in question—the Netherlands Indies, Surinam, and Curaçao.

From dependencies of the kingdom they had become its partners within the framework of the Netherlands realm.

On September 6, 1938, the nation celebrated the fortieth anniversary of Queen Wilhelmina's inauguration. Though she seemed to have shunned rather than sought popularity, she was then no less close to the hearts of the people than when she appealed to their loyalty as a winsome young girl just come of age. For they knew that the forty years of her reign had been spent in devoted service to the country. A constitutional monarch's task, self-effacing though it be, is nevertheless no sinecure. The law is the royal will defined with the co-operation of the States-General, and that being so, the queen never shirked her share in the partnership. Posterity will speak of her reign as the Age of Wilhelmina, and the phrase will not be an empty flattery. Her earnest devotion to duty and the example she set in stressing spiritual above material values informed the period of her rule with dignity and restraint.

Her country, in the late thirties, was a model of well-organized social life. There were no glaring contrasts between excessive wealth and abject poverty. The land was dotted with prosperous villages and towns whose inhabitants, made mobile by bicycles and automobiles, built their homes ever farther away from the centers, until the countryside, especially in the densely populated western part, began to assume the aspect of a huge garden city. Co-operatives flourished in the agricultural districts and made it possible for the individual farmer, however far removed from any urban center, to dispose of his dairy and agricultural products at prices that gave him an ample compensation for his labors. The working classes enjoyed more leisure than in former days. People with limited incomes joined travel societies which organized cheap excursion trips to England, France, Germany or Switzerland, and enriched the travelers' minds with impressions and experiences that used to be the exclusive privileges of the rich. Half a century ago, when skating and sailing were the only popular sports, most Hollanders found their pleasures at home. In the late thirties the out-of-doors had become the natural habitat of the Dutch. The North Sea beaches swarmed in summer with bathers, boys' and girls' camps were scattered all over the country, and youth hostels offered hikers and cyclists shelter for the night at low prices. As a consequence the general health of the nation greatly improved during the past decades. Infant mortality was very low. And although the birth rate decreased, the annual increase of the population exceeded the one hundred thousand mark. Next to Belgium, Holland was the most densely populated country of Europe. If Hitler was looking for *Lebensraum* for his German people, he had no need to look for it in Holland.

On May 10, 1940 his hordes invaded this happy land and despoiled it of its charm. He could not destroy the country's beauty, however. Its low-lying pasture land dotted with farmsteads and windmills and cattle is still a painter's paradise. But the livestock was decimated and was no longer a ubiquitous adornment of the landscape. Prosperity went the way of liberty. The Nazis looted the country of foodstuffs and commodities. Everything was rationed and many things for which one held the indispensable ration cards were not obtainable. Clothing could not be renewed, and leather became so scarce that many Hollanders exchanged their wornout footwear for the wooden shoes of more primitive days. Malnutrition and undernourishment showed their evil effects on the general health. Skin and eye diseases were prevalent. Little children fainted in the classrooms and were taken home to despairing parents. Fuel was just as scarce as food, and neighboring families assembled on frosty days around a joint fireplace. Where bombs had not fallen, the old town houses and the more modern homes in the suburbs and the countryside still looked like their former selves. But the joy had gone out of them, and the lack of a fresh coat of paint—once the pride of every house owner—was symbolic of that inner lack of cheer.

The freedom of unguarded speech was gone. A Hollander used to express himself without fear on all subjects under the sun. That has been his good right from time immemorial. He could not get accustomed to the reticence enforced by the Gestapo. The universities of Leyden and Delft were closed in punishment of the students' recalcitrance. The others remained open, but practically ceased to function, if the function of a university be to encourage the free exchange of ideas and independence of thinking. The Dutch press, once proud of its outspokenness, became a dummy on the knees of the ventriloquist Goebbels. The Dutchman lost all interest in his daily paper except for what it told him about the latest food regulations. He listened to the radio, not the fake one that Goebbels fed with his lies, but the forbidden broadcasts from London and New York; imprisonment was the penalty, but everyone was willing to risk his freedom for a message from the lands of the free.

But the theme of this book is the making of modern Holland. How Hitler's hordes unmade it should not form part of her story. At the time of the German occupation the Führer proclaimed that the Netherlands had been reunited with the Reich. On another occasion he informed the world that the new order he was creating was destined to last for the next one thousand years. The Dutch were told to look forward to a millennium of life under German rule.

That is, to put it mildly, not a very pleasant prospect. But there is comfort in the reminder that such promises of a coming millennium have often been vainly made in the past. The trusting innocents who waited and prepared themselves for its coming were always disappointed in their hope. Besides, human history, in comparison to the age of this earth, is the record of but a brief span of time, and one thousand years, in comparison to that record, is excessively long. The millennium that preceded the one that Hitler claims to have inaugurated covers nearly the entire history of the Netherlands. This little book recounts the succession of changes, gradual and violent, that turned the Dutch people, once enslaved by the Vikings, into an independent, prosperous, and self-confident nation. In the millennium of self-rule that dawned for the Netherlands around the year one thousand, the tyrannies of Philip II, Louis XIV, and Napoleon were but incidents. When the Japanese call their war in China an incident they are more truthful than they mean to be; the mighty flow of Chinese history is temporarily disturbed by a volcanic eruption, but divine omniscience sees it rolling on unchecked to a better future. Even thus the invasion of so many national territories by Hitler's armies is but an incident in the history of the several nations. If they were not sure of that in their distress, they might not find the strength to suffer and passively resist. The Dutch endure their present plight convinced that Hitler's power will crumble. When that happens, the stream of Dutch history, temporarily dammed and deflected by Nazi interference, will return to the bed which its free flow has cut across the ages.

Index

Abjuration of the sovereign, 80
Act of Consultation, 162
Act of Seclusion, 111
Adagia of Erasmus, 52
Adams, John, first Envoy of the U.S.A. at The Hague, 168
Agrarian Law of the Dutch East Indies, 195
Agriculture, 212
Albert, Archduke of Austria, 90
Albert, Duke of Bavaria, Count of Holland, 30
Aleander, Jerome, 47
Alkmaar, 73
Alpine race, 12
Alva, Duke of, 65, 69, 71-75, 83, 88
Amalia of Solms, wife of Prince Frederick Henry, 118
Amboina massacre, 99, 109, 111
Amsterdam, 51, 76, 104, 112, 113, 129, 131, 139, 168, 176, 200, *et passim*
Anabaptists, 61
Anne, Queen of England, 133, 134
Anne of Hannover, Princess of Orange, 161
Antirevolutionaries, 189, 192, 203
Antwerp, 50, 69, 71, 83
Apology of Prince William of Orange, 79
Arabic taught at Leyden, 143
Arminians, 91, 93, 94, 146, 148
Arminius, Jacobus, 91
Army reform, 87-88, 204-205
Arnolfini, John, 52
Art, 52-55, 149-152, 155, 198
Artevelde, Jacob van, 24-25
Artois, 40
Arts and crafts, 53, 150
Atjeh, 196
Augsburg, *see* Diet of
Australia, 145
Austria, 129, 156, 204
Austrian Netherlands, 159, 171, 179
Autonomy in the East Indies, 210
Aviation, 211

Balance of power, 125
Baltic trade, 51, 112
Ban and edict, 78
Barents, Willem, 96
Barrier towns, 136, 159, 160, 168

Barrier Treaty, 136-137, 156
Batavi, 172
Batavia, 98, 145, 209
Batavian legion, 172
Batavian Republic, 172-175, 192
Battles of: Denain, 135; Four Days', 116; Kortrijk (Courtray), 23; Leipzig, 178; Lützen, 101; Nancy, 38; Nördlingen, 101; Sluis, 24; the Downs, 100, 109
Beast epic, 28
Bede (a request for a levy), 36, 63
Beggary, 140
Bekker, Balthazar, 146
Belgium, 182, 206
Bentheim, H. L., 141
Berlage, H. P., 200
Betoverde Wereld, 146
Bible, 60-61, 94, 149
Bijltjesdag, 178-179
Bilderdijk, Willem, 175, 186
Birth rate, 213
Blake, Robert, 110
Boehme, Jacob, 147
Boerhaave, Hermannus, 143
Bois-le-Duc, 101
Bonaparte, Louis, King of Holland, 174-176
Bonn, 125
Borneo, 193
Bosch, Jerome, 54
Bouts, Dirc, 54
Boxer Rebellion, 204
Brabant, 20
Brandenburg, 127, 129-130
Brazil, 97
Bread-and-Cheese Rabble, 59
Bredero, Gerbrand Adriaenszoon, 149
Brielle, or The Brill, 72, 83, 99
Brotherhood of the Common Life, 43, 60
Brueghel, Peter, 54
Bruges, 22, 24, 37, 47, 50, 83
Brugman, Johannes, 43
Brussels, 40, 83, 182
Burghers, 18
Burgundian kreis, 41, 102

Calvinism, 62, 66, 107, 186
Calvin's Presbyterian polity adopted at Wesel, 66

INDEX

Cambray, 42
Canary Islands, 51
Cape Horn, 144
Carolingians, 17
Carrying trade, 51, 84, 139, 169, 184
Caton, William, 147
Cats, Jakob, 148-149
Caveat emptor, 50
Censorship, 107
Centre, the Roman Catholic party, 190
Chamber of Accounts, 37, 87
Chambers of Rhetoric, 57
Charlemagne, 16
Charles I, King of England, 80, 100, 104, 109
Charles II, King of England, 113, 117, 119-121, 127-131, 138
Charles II, King of Spain, 132
Charles V, King of Spain, Emperor of Germany, 39-42, 47, 49, 54, 56, 62, 63, 65
Charles VI, Emperor, 159
Charles IX, King of France, 76
Charles X, King of Sweden, 112
Charles Albert, Elector of Bavaria, 159
Charles, Archduke of Austria, pretender to the Spanish throne, 134, 135
Charles Martel, 16
Charles the Bold, Duke of Burgundy, 33, 36-38
Chaucer, Geoffrey, 21, 43
Chièvres, Count of, 47
Child, Sir Josiah, 142
Child of State, 118-119, 121, 124
Chlodowech, King of the Franks, 15
Christian Historicals, 189, 199
Christian school, 190
Churchill, John, Earl, later Duke of Marlborough, 134
Civic guards, 87
Classis, 66
Cleanliness, 142
Cloth industry, 50, 139
Codfish (a political faction in Holland), 30, 59
Coen, Jan Pieterszoon, 98
Colijn, Hendrikus, 204, 208
College of Montaigu, 46
Collegiants, 147
Colloquies of Erasmus, 46
Cologne, 52, 66, 121, 125
Colonial enterprise, 89, 96-99, 145, 156, 193, 208
Comites, 18
Commerce, 19, 50, 51, 88

Communist party, 199
Compromise, 67
Compulsory insurance of workers against disability, 199
Condé, Prince of, 121
Confession of faith, 66
Consistory, 66
Continental system, 178
Contraband, 110, 127, 167
Co-operatives, 212
Copenhagen, 112
Co-prosperity sphere, 209
Cort van der Linden, P. W. A., 203
Council of Department Heads, 210
Council of State, 40, 63, 67, 68, 83, 85-87, *et passim*
Court of Holland, 37
Courtray, 23
Cromwell, Oliver, 110, 111, 113
Curaçao, 97, 165, 184, 211
Cusa, Nicholas, 45

Da Costa, Isaac, 186, 189
Daendels, Herman Willem, 172, 175, 192
Dairy products, 212
Danzig, 112
David, Gerard, 54
David of Burgundy, Bishop of Utrecht, 33
De Celles, Count, 177, 178
Declaration of Independence, 80, 163
Deflation, 208
De Graeff, Johannes, 166
De Groot, Pieter, 119
De Hooch, Pieter, 149, 152
De Houtman, Cornelis, 88-89
De Jure Belli ac Pacis of Hugo Grotius, 125
Deken, Agatha, 155
Dekker, Eduard Douwes, *see* Multatuli
De Labadie, Jean, 147
De Lairesse, Gerard, 155
Delft potteries, 139
Delft university, 214
De Nederlandsche Spectator, 155
Denmark, 112, 127, 129
De Parival, J. N., 141
De Requesens, Don Louis, 75
De Ruyter, Michiel Adriaenszoon, 111, 113-117, 126-128, 141
Devaluation, 208
Deventer, 44
De Witt, Cornelis, 122
De Witt, Jan, 106-123, 141

INDEX

Diepenveen, 45
Diet of Augsburg, 41
Dillenburg, 64
Dordrecht, 75, 139
Drinking, 141
Dryden, John, 99
Dudley, Robert, Earl of Leicester, 84
Dumouriez, Ch. F. D., 171-172
Dunkirk, 128
Dürer, Albrecht, 53
Dutch, origin of the name, 17; a term of abuse, 109
Dutch East India Company, 89, 98, 139, 192-193
Dutch language, 38
Dutch Reformed Church, 66, 94, 107, 144, 146, 147, 163, 186, 190
Dutch Republic, 40, 78, 85, 86, 87, 102, et passim
Dutch West India Company, 89, 96, 113, 139, 166

East Indies Administration Act (1925), 210
East Indies Government Act (1854), 194
Ecclesiastical reform, 42
Edict of Nantes revoked by Louis XIV, 130
Education, 58, 142, 203
Edward I, King of England, 22
Edward III, King of England, 24
Egmont, Lamoraal, Count of, 71
Elckerlijc, 57
Electoral Law, 202
Elisabeth, Duchess of Bavaria, 33
Elizabeth, Queen of England, 82, 99
Emden, 66
Emigration to America, 187
Emma, Queen Regent, 197
Enkhuizen, 51
Erasmus, 46-48, 107, 143
Erpenius, Thomas, 143
Eternal Edict, 119, 121
Eugene, Prince of Savoy, 134
Evelyn, John, 140
Evertsen, Johan, 114
Everyman, 57
Exploration, 144

Farnese, Alexander, Prince of Parma, 83-85
Federal Synod of Dordrecht, 94
Federalists, 174
Ferdinand of Aragon, 39

Feudalism, 19, 28, 34, 37, 59, 193
First Chamber, 188, 197
Fishing rights in English waters, 109, 110, 113, 127
Flanders, 20-25, 40
Flemish, 181
Floris V, Count of Holland, 22
Flushing, 65, 83, 100
Forced cultivation system, 194
Franche-Comté, 118
Francis I, King of France, 41
Franks, 12
Frederick III, King of Denmark, 112
Frederick Henry, Prince of Orange, 100, 104
Frederick William II, King of Prussia, 171
Free trade, 89, 110, 209
Free University on Reformed Principles, 189
Freedom, the extramural territory of a town, 26
Freedom of the seas, 110
French fashions, 155
French school, 143
Friesland, 20, 125, 130
Frieze, 22
Frisians, 12-16, 20, 21, 39
Furniture, 52

Geertgen tot St. Jans, 54
Gelderland, 20, 34, 39
Germanic, 12
Gestapo, 214
Geus, 68
Ghent, 22, 24, 25, 40, 50, 83
Gibraltar, 134, 137
Gobius, J. F., 143
Goebbels, P. J., 214
Gold Coast, 113-114
Gold standard, 208
Golden Age of the Netherlands, 138-152
Gomarists, 91
Gomarus, Franciscus, 91
Gossaert, Jan, called Mabuse, 54
Gouda, 139
Governor general of the East Indies, 210
Grain trade, 88
Grand Alliance, 132, 135
Granvelle, *see* Perrenot
Grave, 85
Great Assembly, 105
Great Privilege, 38

INDEX

Groen van Prinsterer, Guillaume, 189
Groningen, 125
Groote, Geert, 44-46
Grotius, Hugo, 84, 86, 92, 125, 143
Guicciardini, Lodovico, 52, 55, 58, 59
Guilder, 208
Guilds, 50, 57
Gustavus Adolphus, King of Sweden, 100-101
Guy of Dampierre, Count of Flanders, 22

Haarlem, 54, 72, 139; linens manufactured at, 139
Haarlem Lake reclaimed, 206
Haec Libertatis ergo, 73
Hainaut, 31, 33
Hals, Frans, 149, 152
Handicrafts, 53
Harris, Sir James, 171
Heemskerk, Th., 204
Heerendiensten, 195
Heidelberg catechism, 66
Heinsius, Anthony, 132, 158
Henrietta, Duchess of Orleans, 119
Henry II, King of France, 65
Henry III, King of France, 82
Henry V, King of England, 32
Henry Casimir, Stadtholder of Friesland, 130-131, 133
Herring trade, 51, 139
Heyn, Piet, 98
Hirohito, Emperor of Japan, 210
Hitler, Adolf, 206, 213, 214
Hogerbeets, Rombout, 93
Holland, County of, 20, 84, 85, 87, 92, 94-95, 102, 105, 106, 111, 171; Kingdom of, 175
Holland (Michigan), 187
Holy Roman Empire, 17
Hooft, Pieter Corneliszoon, 108, 149
Hooks (a political faction in Holland), 30, 33, 59
Hoorn, 51
Hoorne, Count of, 71
Housing, 200
Howell, James, 140
Hudson, Henry, 96-97
Huguenots, 76, 100, 130, 139
Humphrey, Duke of Gloucester, 32, 33
Hundred Years' War, 29
Hunebeds, 11
Hutten, Ulrich von, 47
Huygens, Christian, 144
Huygens, Constantijn, 149

Iconoclastic riots, 69
IJsel, 15, 20, 46
Imitatio Christi, 45-46
Individualism, 24, 42
Industrial revolution, 191, 199
Industries, 139
Infant mortality, 213
Inquisition, 66, 68, 73
Institutes of the Christian Religion, 70
International law, 125, 205
Invasion, effects of, 213-214
Isabel, Infanta of Spain, 90, 101
Isabella of Castile, 39
Isabella of Portugal, wife of Philip the Good of Burgundy, 37

Jacoba, Countess of Holland, Zeeland, and Hainaut, 30-34
James I, King of England, 99
James II, King of England, 131, 133
Jan Beukelszoon of Biervliet, 51
Jan Beukelszoon of Leyden, 61
Jan Mathysen, 61
Japan, 208-210
Java, 88, 98, 145, 193, 194, 208
Java sugar, 208
Jews, 97, 145
Joanna, wife of Philip the Fair, Duke of Burgundy, 39
Joanna, Duchess of Brabant, 30
John, Count of Nassau, 78
John, Duke of Bavaria, 31, 32, 33, 53
John IV, Duke of Brabant, 31
John Maurice, Count of Nassau, governor of Brazil, 97-98
John the Fearless, Duke of Burgundy, 30
John William Friso, 133
Jones, John Paul, 169
Joseph I, Emperor, 135
Joseph II, Emperor, 168
Josken de Prez, 55
Jus de non evocando, 27, 36
Justification through faith, 60

Kampen, 51
Kelto-Slavic race, 12
Keurmede, 59
Knights of the Golden Fleece, 38, 63, 67, 68
Kobe conference (1934), 209
Kortrijk, 23
Kuyper, Abraham, 189

INDEX

Labor party, 199, 203
Lamb, Charles, 147
La Muette de Portici, 181
Landjuweel, 57
Landscape painting, 54, 151, 155
Landstorm, 205
La Rochelle, 100
Lasso, Orlando, 55
Latin, influence of on the Dutch language, 14; school, 143
Lawrence, Henry, 167
League of Armed Neutrality, 167
Lebensraum, 213
Lebrun, Charles François, 177, 178
Leechwater, Jan Adriaenszoon, 140
Lely, C., 204, 205
Leo X, Pope, 47
Leopold I, King of the Belgians, 183
Les Délices de la Hollande, 141
Lessing, G. E., 151
Lewis Ernest, Duke of Brunswick-Wolfenbüttel, 161-169
Leyden, 73, 74, 139
Liberals, 187-192, 199
Limburg, 101, 190
Limited convoy, 167
Literature, 27, 28, 56, 155; mystic, 44-45, 57
Loevesteyn Castle, 109
London, 66, 117
Lord Advocate of Holland, 82, 95
Lothair, 17
Lotharingia, 17
Loudon, Jonkheer J., 203, 205
Louis the Bavarian, 30
Louis XIV, King of France, 116, 117, 118
Louis XVI, King of France, 80
Louis of Male, Count of Flanders, 30
Louis, Count of Nassau, 67, 70
Louis of Nevers, Count of Flanders, 24, 29
Louvain, 37, 48
Lower Lotharingia, 20-21, 34
Luther, Martin, 47-48, 60, 62
Lutherans, 70, 145
Luxemburg, 33, 130, 131

Maastricht, 52, 101, 129
Maatschappij van Weldadigheid, 184
Mabuse, *see* Gossaert
Macassar, 145
Malacca, 145, 196
Malay Archipelago, 192-196
Manhattan, 96-97, 145

Margaret, Duchess of Parma, 67
Margaret, Duchess of Savoy, 58
Maria Theresa, 156, 159
Market rights, 26
Martyrs of the Reformation, 61
Mary, Duchess of Burgundy, 38
Mary of Nimmegen, 56-57
Mary Stuart, wife of Prince William II of Orange, 109
Mary Stuart, wife of Prince William III of Orange, 128, 131
Mason, Sir John, 49
Mataram, 145
Maurice, Prince of Orange, 86-96
Max Havelaar, 194
Maximilian of Hapsburg, Emperor, 39, 50
Mazarin, 103
Mechelen, 37, 40, 42, 83
Mediterranean, 88, 127
Medway, 117, 120
Memlinc, Hans, 54
Menno Simonsz, 61
Mennonism, 61-62, 147
Messina, 127
Mexico, 49
Minahassa, 193
Ministerial responsibility, 188
Minuit, Peter, 97
Modern Devotion, 44, 46, 52, 58, 60
Molitor, G. J. J., 177
Moluccas, 88, 98, 145, 193
Monarchical power, 104, 106, 176
Monck, George, Duke of Albemarle, 116
Monopolies, 89
Montague, Lady Mary Wortley, 140
Montaigu, College of, 46
Montanus, Petrus, 59
Mor, Anton (called Antonio Moro), 56
Morus, Thomas, 47
Multatuli, pen name of Eduard Douwes Dekker, 194
Münster in Westphalia, 61, 102, 121, 125
Music, 55, 146
Mystery plays, 56

Naarden, 72
Napoleon, 174-179
Napoleonic Empire, 177
National Assembly, 174
National Congress of Belgium, 182
Nationalism, awakening of, 23
Navigation Act, 110, 113, 117

INDEX

Navy reform, 116
Netherlands Bank, 184
Netherlands Trading Society, 184
Neutral primary school, 184, 190
New Amsterdam, 96-97, 145
New Jerusalem at Münster, 61
New Netherland, 113, 117, 127, 145
Nicholas II, Czar of Russia, 204
Nobility, 59, 67, 185
Noblesse de robe, 37, 67
North Brabant, 190
Novaya Zemlya, 96

Obrecht, Jacob, 55
Observance, 43
Okeghen, Joannes, 55
Oligarchy, 107-108, 126, 130, 158, 160
Olinda, 97
Open-door policy in the East Indies, 209
Orange, House of, 111, 122, 130, 164, 170, 171, 178, 185, 200, *et passim*
Orangists, 118, 119, 159, 161, 170
Order of the Golden Fleece, 37
Oslo Convention, 207
Osnabrück, 103
Ostend Company, 156, 159
Ottawa Agreements of 1932, 207
Otto I, Emperor, 17
Oudinot, N. Ch., Duke of Reggio, 176
Overbury, Sir Thomas, 141

Pacification of Ghent, 78, 81
Painting, 52-55, 149-151, 155, 198
Parker, Sir Hyde, 168
Parma, *see* Farnese
Patrimonial provinces, 39, 49, 63
Patriots, 168, 174, 185, 187
Pauperism, 191
Pax Dei, 20
Peace conferences, 204
Pearl Harbor, 209
Peasantry, 59
Pella (Iowa), 187
Pensionary, 95
Pepin, 16
Periwig Period, 153-172
Perrenot, Anthony, Lord of Granvelle, 49, 67
Peru, 49
Peutinger, Konrad, 47
Philip II, King of Spain, 42, 49, 63, 65, 67, 71, 90
Philip III, King of Spain, 90
Philip V, King of Spain, 132, 135

Philip the Bold, Duke of Burgundy, 30
Philip the Fair, King of France, 22
Philip the Fair, Duke of Burgundy, 39
Philip the Good, Duke of Burgundy, 30-37, 39, 53
Pichegru, Charles, 172
Pietism, 146
Poland, 127
Polders reclaimed, 140
Population, 138
Portugal, 88, 98, 112
Pragmatic Sanction (1724), 159
Predestination, 91, 148
Prehistoric man, 1
Primary Education Act, 174
Printing, 58
Privy Council, 37, 38, 40, 63, 68
Proletariat, 185, 192
Proportional representation, 202
Provincial States, 86

Quakers, 145, 147

Raad van Indië, 210
Radbod, King of the Frisians, 16
Raffles, Sir Thomas Stamford, 192-194
Railways, 184
Rammekens, 83, 100
Recife, 97
Reformation, 66
Regents for the King of Spain in the Netherlands: Albert of Austria, 90; Duke of Alva, 65, 69, 71-75, 83, 88; Louis de Requesens, 75; Margaret of Parma, 67; Margaret of Savoy, 58; Prince of Parma, 83-85
Rembrandt Harmenszoon van Ryn, 149-152
René, Count of Nassau, Prince of Orange, 64
Réveil, 186, 189
Revivalism, 186
Revolt, its justice debated, 70
Reynard the Fox, 28
Rhode Island, 144
Richelieu, 100, 128
Right of amendment, 188
Right of search at sea, 127
Rijnsburg, 146-147
Robinson Crusoe, 155
Roermond, 101
Rogers, Woodes, 145
Roman Catholics, 147, 190, 203
Romances of chivalry, 27
Romans, 13-15

INDEX

Rotterdam, 140, 206
Rousseau, Jean Jacques, 163
Royal African Company, 113
Rubens, Peter Paul, 149
Russia, 88, 167, 178
Ruusbroec, Jacob van, 44

St. Augustine, 45
St. Bartholomew's Day massacre, 76
St. Eustatius, 97, 165
St. Francis, 43
St. George del Mina, 97
Salt works, 51
Salute of the flag, 110, 111
Saxons, 12
Scheldt, 83, 206
Schimmelpenninck, Rutger Jan, 174-175
Scholte, H. P., 187
Schultens, Albert, 143
Science, 143-144, 154
Sea Beggars, 72, 114
Second Chamber, 188, 194, 197, 202, 203
Sewel, Judith, 147
Sewel, Willem, 147
Sigismund, Emperor, 30, 31
Sluis, 24, 85
South African War, 204
Sovereignty, 84, 85, 91, 126, 163
Spanish Netherlands, 116, 117, 118, 128, 131, 132, 13.
Spinoza, Baruch, 144, 147
Spitsbergen, 96, 144
Stadtholders, lieutenant governors of the Burgundian dukes, 37, 86; in the Republic appointees of the provincial States, 86
Standonck, Johannes, 46
State pensions for the aged, widows, and orphans, 199
State universities, 184
Staten Island, 144
States Bible, 94
States-General, 36, 38, 39, 49, 63, 65, 79, 82, *et passim*
States' rights, 92
Steamship companies, 184
Steen, Jan, 142
Stevin, Simon, 143, 144
Still life painting, 151
Strada, Famiano, 80
Stuyvesant, Peter, 113, 145
Suffering Church, 189
Suffrage, 191, 202

Sumatra, 193, 196
Supreme Court, 37, 38
Surinam, 117, 211
Suyono, Pangeran Ario, 211
Swammerdam, Jacob, 144
Sweden, 112, 127, 129-130
Swift, Jonathan, 136

Tacitus, 13, 15, 172
Tangier, 204
Tasman, Abel, 144
Tasmania, 144
Tax farming abolished, 161
Temple, Sir William, 118, 138, 141, 142
Ten days' campaign, 183
Ternate, 145
Terps, 14
The Dutch Drawn to the Life, 141
The Hague, 40, 85
The Tragedy of Sir John van Oldenbarnevelt, 142
The World Turn'd Upside Down, 146
Theater, 146, 154
Thietmar von Merseburg, 18
Thomas à Kempis, 45
Thorbecke, Jan Rudolf, 188-192
Three Days' Revolution in Paris, 181
Tokyo, 209
Tolerance, 76
Towns, origin of, 18-27
Trade unions, 200
Trading with the enemy, 84
Treaties of: Aix-la-Chapelle (1668), 118; (1748), 160; Breda (1667), 117, 120; Cateau Cambrésis (1559), 63, 65; Dover (1670), 120; Elbing (1656), 112; London (1831), 183; Nijmegen (1678), 129, 130; Paris (1784), 169; Pyrenees (1659), 125; Roskilde (1658), 112; Ryswick (1697), 131, 133; The Hague (1701), 132-133; Utrecht (1713), 135-137, 153, 156; Verdun (843), 16; Westminster (1654), 110, 112; (1674), 127; Westphalia (1648), 103, 130
Trekschuit, 184
Treub, M. W. F., 203
Triple Alliance, 118-119
Troelstra, Pieter Jelle, 199, 203
Tromp, Cornelis, 111, 114, 116, 117, 122, 126
Tromp, Marten Harpertszoon, 100, 110
True Freedom, 107, 122

INDEX

Turenne, Henri de la Tour d'Auvergne, vicomte de, 121
Twelve Years' Truce (1609–1621), 89, 93, 95

Unemployment Council, 200
Union of Utrecht, 78, 81, 85, 172, 190
Unitarists, 174
United States of America, 164, 197
University of Leyden, 74, 143, 214
Usselincx, Willem, 89, 96
Utrecht, 20, 42, 84, 92-93, 170

Van Bleiswyk, Pieter, 165
Van Bylandt, F. S., Count, 167
Van den Bosch, Johannes, 194
Van den Vondel, Joost, 148
Van der Capellen tot den Poll, Baron Joan Derk, 164, 170
Van der Duyn van Maasdam, A. F. T. A., 179
Van der Heim, Anthony, 158
Van der Hulst, François, 48
Van der Werff, Adriaan, 74
Van der Weyden, Roger, 56
Van Diemen's Land, 144
Van Effen, Justus, 155
Van Eyck, Jan, 52
Van Ghent, Joseph, 117
Van Ginneken, J., 46
Van Hogendorp, Gysbert Karel, 164, 179, 184
Van Hout, Jan, 74
Van Leeuwenhoek, Anton, 144, 152
Van Leyden, Lucas, 54
Van Limburg-Stirum, Leopold, Count, 179
Van Maerlant, Jacob, 27, 56
Van Mander, Carel, 151
Van Marnix, John, 67
Van Marnix, Philip, 67, 76
Van Oldenbarnevelt, Johan, 82, 84-95, 99, 105, 106
Van Raalte, A. C., 187
Van Ruysdael, Jacob, 152
Van Schuurman, Anna Maria, 147
Van Scorel, Jan, 56
Van Slingelandt, Simon, 156-158
Van Wassenaar-Obdam, Jacob, 114
Venlo, 85, 101
Vermeer, Johannes, 149, 152
Viking raids, 17-18
Vives, Juan Luis, 47

Volksraad, 210
Von Waldeck, Count, 125

Waardgelders, 92
Walcheren, Isle of, 120
Walloon provinces, 181
War of classes, 192
Welfare legislation, 199
Wenceslaus, Duke of Luxemburg, 30
Wesel, 66
West Germanic, 12
West Indies, 132
Whaling industry, 139
Wilhelmina, Queen of the Netherlands, 198-213
Wilhelmina of Prussia, wife of Prince William V of Orange, 162, 171
Willem, Flemish poet, 28
William I, King of the Netherlands, 179-187, 194
William II, King of the Netherlands, 186-188
William III, King of the Netherlands, 187, 189, 197
William II, Count of Holland, 21
William V, Count of Holland, 30
William VI, Count of Holland, 30, 31
William, Prince of Orange, 64, 67, 69-80, 82, 86, 104, 122
William II, Prince of Orange, 104, 109
William III, Prince of Orange, 118, 121, 124-133
William IV, Prince of Orange, 159-161
William V, Prince of Orange, 162-172
William Louis, Count of Nassau, 86
William of Ostrevant, 30
Willibrord, 15
Windesheim congregation, 45-46
Witchcraft, 146
Wolff-Bekker, Elizabeth, 155
Women's social status, 142
Wool imports from England, 22
World War I, 205

Yorke, Sir Robert, 165
Ypres, 22, 24, 50, 83

Zeeland, 12, 115, 176
Zoutman, Johan Arnold, 168
Zuider Zee, 140, 205-206
Zutphen, 72, 85
Zwolle, 51

AUGSBURG COLLEGE AND SEMINARY
LIBRARY - MINNEAPOLIS 4, MINN.